Getting Down to Business

Dr. Bruce C. Johnson, Ph.D., MBA
Patricia D. Lesko, MFA, Editor

First Edition

To order, contact:

The Part-Time Press

P.O. Box 130117

Ann Arbor, MI 48113-0117

www.Part-TimePress.com

orders@part-timepress.com

Phone: 734-930-6854

Fax: 734-665-9001

First Printing: October 2015

© 2015 The Part-Time Press

ISBN: 978-0-940017-13-9 (paperback)

Printed in the United States of America

Table of Contents

Preface to the First Edition 8

Introduction 9

    Helpful Tips: "If You Don't Have Jitters On the First Day, Maybe You Shouldn't Be Teaching" 11

How to Get the Most Out of This Book 12

CHAPTER 1—TEACHING BUSINESS: WHAT IT'S ALL ABOUT

Orientation to College & Adult Teaching 13

What Business Students Need 15

Business Basics 16

    Case Studies 17

    Research Methodologies..17

    Field Trips and Guest Lecturers..18

Establishing a Teaching Environment..18

    Characteristics of Good Teaching 21

    Setting the Tone 22

    Teachers as Actors and Actresses..22

Classroom Communication..23

The Three R's of Teaching 24

Teaching Styles 25

Professional Ethics..27

    Ethics and the Business Instructor 28

    Ethics and the Profession..28

    Professional Ethics and Students 29

Academic Dishonesty 31

Checklist for Part-Time Faculty..32

CHAPTER 2—ALL ABOUT ADULT STUDENTS

Why Trust Matters 34

Meeting Students' Needs 35

Getting Students Engaged in the Process of Learning................35

Andragogy: The Essence of an Adult Learner 37

Student Learning Styles 38

Assessing Learning Styles 40

    Myers-Brigg..40

    VARK..40

    Multiple Intelligences 40

    Kolb Learning Style Inventory 41

Self-Directed (Student-Centered) Learning..............................41

Acquisition and Creation of Knowledge....................................42

Adult Student Diversity 45

Cognitive Development and Bloom's Taxonomy 46
Critical Thinking 48
Transformational Learning 50
    Defining Student Motivation 51
    Internal and External Motivation 52
Maslow's Heirarchy of Needs in the Classroom....................................53
"Rubrics and Adult Learners: Andragogy and Assessment"...................57

CHAPTER 3—STUDENT ENGAGEMENT—WHY IT MATTERS

Student Retention—Why It Matters 58
    Students Make the First Choice 59
    Instructors Reaffirm or Negate that Choice 59
    Retention is More Than Numbers...59
Student Engagement 101 60
    Defining Student Engagement 61
    The Instructor's Role in Student Engagement 62
Encouraging Student Engagement 63
Demonstrate Engagement for Your Students 63
"Unmasking the Effects of Student Engagement on First-Year College
    Grades and Persistance" 65

CHAPTER 4—EFFECTIVE STRATEGIES FOR TEACHING ADULTS

Teacher Behaviors...66
Teacher Roles in a Collaborative Classroom 67
Facilitation vs. Teaching 68
Student Behaviors 69
Communication and Tone 71
Developing Strong Working Relationships...73
Time Management Strategies...75

CHAPTER 5—COMMUNICATING WITH STUDENTS

Keep Information Flowing...78
    Blogs 78
    Twitter...79
    Creative Ways to Use Twitter in the Business Classroom 80
    Social Networking Sites 81
Learning Management Systems 81
Second Life 81
Student Response Systems...82

CHAPTER 6—CLASSROOM TEACHING TECHNIQUES

Classroom Teaching Techniques...86

Instructor-Based Techniques 87
Student-Based Techniques 87
Out-of-Class Activities 87
The Lecture 87
Discussion 92
Discussion Facilitation Strategies 92
Discussions in the Business Classroom 94
Group Projects—A Must in the Business Classroom 95
Classroom Conflict: Prevention and Resolution 96

CHAPTER 7—PREPARING FOR THE FIRST CLASS

Class Preparation Checklist 98
Planning Your Business Course—In A Hurry 99
The Course Syllabus 101
The Lesson Plan 106
Course Objectives 108
Use Supplemental Materials 108
Policies 109
Surviving the First Class 111
"Jitters. Butterflies. Nerves." 113

CHAPTER 8—TEACHING LARGE CLASSES

The Lecture Hall 115
Administration 116
Keeping Students Engaged 117
Facilitating Discussions in Large Classes 119
Tests and Assignments 121
Tips for Teaching Large Classes and Lectures 122
Resources for Teaching Large Classes 123

CHAPTER 9—BUSINESS STUDENTS AND WRITING

Developing Written Assignments with a Purpose 124
A Step-By-Step Approach to Building Assignments 125
Step One: Learning Objectives 125
Step Two: Identifying a Purpose 126
Step Three: Determine Possible Outcomes 127
Step Four: Developing Instructions 127
Step Five: Develop a Rubric 127
Utilizing Rubrics 128
Formative vs. Summative Assessments 130
"Student Writing: Old Habits Die Hard and Other Clichés" 131

Grading Written Assignments 132
Feedback 133

CHAPTER 10—TESTS, TESTING AND ASSIGNING GRADES

Tests and Testing 135
Tests/Question Types 135
    Essay Tests/Questions 135
    Multiple Choice Questions 136
    Recall and Completion Tests/Questions 137
What Do Grades Really Measure? 137
    Grading: The Basics 139
    Evaluation Plan 140

CHAPTER 11—TEACHING WITH TECHNOLOGY

Learning to Embrace Technological Tools 142
Technology Enhances Learning 143
Classroom Presentation Software 144
Software Applications That Enhance Learning 144
Integrating Social Networking Into Classroom Facilitation 145
"Don't Poke Me: Professors' Privacy in the Age of Facebook" ... 146

CHAPTER 12—TEACHING ONLINE

Getting Started 147
Online Lingo 101 148
Traditional Versus Non-Traditional Biz Students Online 149
Technological Preparation 150
Design and Content Preparation 151
Tips for Working Efficiently 154
Accessibility 155
Community Building 156
Group Work in the Online Classroom 158
Practical Tips for Good Communication in Online Courses 160
A Hybrid Approach to Teaching 161
"Diving Into the Wreck: Revisiting Online Classrooms After the Semester
    Ends" 164

Glossery of Online Terminology 166

References 173
Index 178
Ordering Information 187

Table of Figures

Figure 1.1 — Faculty Checklist 33
Figure 4.1 — Working Relationship Checklist 75
Figure 4.2 — Time Management Review 76
Figure 6.1 — Level of Student Attention 88
Figure 6.2 — Effect of a Pause or Change 89
Figure 7.1 — Class Preparation Checklist 98
Figure 7.2 — Sample Course Syllabus 103
Figure 7.3 — Sample Course Outline 105
Figure 7.4 — Suggested Lesson Plan Format 107
Figure 7.5 — Sample Lesson Plan 107
Figure 7.6 — Sample Grade Review Policy 110
Figure 9.1 — College Level Writing Rubric 129
Figure 10.1 — Evaluation Plan 141

Helpful Tips

"If You Don't Have Jitters On the First Day, Maybe You Shouldn't Be Teaching" by Jenny Ortiz 11

"Rubrics and Adult Learners: Andragogy and Assessment" by Fred C. Bolton 57

"Unmasking the Effects of Student Engagement on First-Year College Grades and Persistance" by George D. Kuh, Ty M. Cruce, Rick Shoup and Jillian Kinzie 65

Creative Ways To Use Twitter In The Business Classroom 80

"Jitters. Butterflies. Nerves." by Melissa Miller, Ed.D 113

Tips for Teaching Large Classes and Lectures 122

Resources for Teaching Large Classes 123

"Student Writing: Old Habits Die Hard and Other Cliches" by Kat Keifer-Newman 131

"Don't Poke Me: Professors' Privacy in the Age of Facebook" by Rich Russell 146

Practical Tips for Good Communication in Online Courses 160

"Diving Into the Wreck: Revisiting Online Classrooms After the Semester Ends" by Rich Russell 164

Preface to the First Edition

I would first like to acknowledge P. D. Lesko and the Part-Time Press for providing me with this exciting opportunity. Everyone has made the process easy to follow, been enjoyable to work with and more importantly they have allowed my work to shine. I appreciate the time and involvement of all who have been associated with the development of this new book.

It is also important to acknowledge those people who have had a positive influence in my journey as an educator and professional writer. The first acknowledgement is for my parents, Dale and Donette, who instilled a love of learning, demonstrated unwavering belief in what I wanted to do with my career, and more importantly taught me about unconditional love through their example.

Next I would like to acknowledge my colleague and friend Kim Eastern (Dr. E), who has provided a source of inspiration, joy, and friendship for a majority of my life. Finally, I want acknowledge my students; past, present, and future, who have created an awakening within me. I do not want to just teach students, I want to inspire them, support their developmental progress, and encourage them to believe in themselves so they will recognize their ability to learn and capacity to do anything they want to accomplish. It is my love of teaching and my passion for writing that bring the greatest meaning to my career.

Dr. J.

Introduction

Business instructors guide the educational pursuits of students already in the workforce. These adult students are seeking formal education as a means of developing their skills, acquiring new skill sets and obtaining knowledge necessary to perform their jobs. They want to prepare for new careers, or advance in their current fields. This handbook offers tools, techniques and adult learning theories to help business instructors facilitate classes, connect with students in meaningful ways and promote student learning. This handbook includes instructional strategies for both the traditional and online classroom environments.

Business instructors bring a real world element to the classroom. They often have experience as leaders in their fields—building teams, coaching, training and mentoring employees. This handbook will help transform instructors into business educators who understand how adults process information and acquire knowledge.

Educating adults is similar to the process of learning; it is adaptive to and reflexive of the needs of students. No one style or method of teaching is applicable for every class or every student. Instructors need a variety of strategies and resources to increase their effectiveness. The purpose of this handbook is to help business instructors develop a set of instructional strategies by providing practical knowledge and insights into how adult business students learn, and how the process of learning occurs within the business classroom—whether that classroom be filled with undergraduate students, graduate students, business majors or non-majors taking a business course.

Getting Down To Business

The Complex Business of Business Courses

Business courses can be theory-driven and include textbooks, technical information, specialized subject matter and general facts. Every business instructor brings with her to the classroom a unique perspective of the business world. The course textbook and materials may dovetail nicely with your background, or may present new information which you'll need to process before teaching the course. In order to bring learning objectives to life for your students, you may also include supplemental sources that are timely and relevant. Information is easily accessible through the Internet and online databases. However, it is always challenging to determine what supplemental materials/information will benefit the class and meet students' professional needs.

Transforming the Business Instructor to Business Educator

Business instructors bring to the class a real-world element based upon extensive knowledge and experience of business theory in practice. Business instructors often have experience as leaders in their fields—experience which includes building teams, coaching and mentoring employees, as well as direct involvement in training and development. In addition, a business instructor's formal education is typically business-based, including business degrees, continuing education classes and training related to business-specific topics. This handbook provides educational concepts about the process of adult learning to enhance the wealth of knowledge and information which business instructors possess.

"If You Don't Have Jitters On the First Day, Maybe You Shouldn't Be Teaching"

by Jenny Ortiz, AdjunctNation.com, originally published September 28, 2011

The work that comes with the first day of classes, as always, feels tedious and only reminds me of the enormous workload I have this coming semester. Like most Freeway Flyers, taking on six classes in one semester is hard and at the end, I tell myself to never to do it again. However, a new semester comes, and with it, the offer to teach some of my favorite courses. Soon I forget the promise I made only a few months earlier, and agree to teach multiple classes on multiple campuses. Ah, such is the life of the Freeway Flyer.

I watch television marathons that revolve around the skills and artistry of cooking, a topic that I rarely mention in my literature classes. Although I knew I had six classes to prep for, I found myself watching massive amounts of "Chopped." The intensity of the competitors kept me glued to the screen. As exciting as a new class can be, there is also that fear that forms in the pit of my stomach. Will this group of students enjoy my class and leave with a better understanding of college reading and writing? Will the semester run smoothly?

These fears will always pop up, no matter how long I've been teaching. Honestly, I hope that they'll always pop up and that I always feel the jittery excitement and nervousness of standing in front of a new class I will be guiding for a brief semester. If I didn't feel any of this, then I'd have to reevaluate my desire to teach. It is not enough to simply do my job.

With all of this in mind, the beginning of a new semester is a time to reevaluate the syllabus, the assignments and any other places in the classroom experience that can be changed and enhanced. This is the start of a new term and new ideas. As I try to communicate with IT about forgotten passwords again, I remember that this is another semester of learning and adapting.

How incredible is that?

Getting Down To Business

How To Get the Most Out of This Book...

One aspect of the book that we hope you'll find useful is the use of icons to highlight important information for the reader.

Keys to Success: Whenever you see this icon, you'll want to take special note because these are tried and true tips to improve your classroom performance.

Caution Light: Whenever you see this icon, you'll know that other successful adjunct and part-time instructors have discovered what NOT to do while teaching.

In addition to the icons, an index has been compiled for ease of use, and we have added a glossary of online terminology. There are chapters on student engagement, teaching online, as well as how to teach students about online research. The table of contents is very detailed to get you to the topic that most interests you at the moment.

Finally, throughout you will find "Helpful Tips." These essays by adjunct faculty address hot button issues such as first day jitters, students and critical thinking, faculty use of social media, and faculty self-evaluation. You will find a list of these essays in the table of contents.

> **This is your quick reference for good teaching. You may use this book as a manual, a guide or for professional reading. It contains practical and informative tips to assist you with your instructional tasks. It is written in a user-friendly manner for your convenience. Enjoy it and GOOD TEACHING.**

CHAPTER 1
TEACHING BUSINESS:
WHAT IT'S ALL ABOUT

Orientation to College and Adult Teaching

In the coming decades, teachers of college and adult students will be faced with many challenges. The influx of multicultural, multi-generational and multilingual students, the impact of technology, online learning and the admission of students with differing academic preparation have demanded the attention of educators. In addition, changing business, economic and political pressures throughout the world have impacted education and, you, the instructor.

You will feel the impact whether you teach in a continuing education program for business/industry or the military; in a liberal arts college with time-honored traditions and values; in a community college with an open door policy; in a public research university with postgraduate programs; or in a distance education program. Your students will be more highly motivated, more challenging and in many ways more enjoyable to teach.

With the focus on accountability and the realization that there are established strategies and techniques for instruction, there is greater emphasis upon quality instruction. Adult students employed in business and industry expect a planned and organized classroom. It is no longer a question of *whether* there are going to be instructional objectives and strategies for teaching; it is a question of *how skilled* instructors are in developing and delivering them.

One of the most important factors, however, remains the human element of teaching. If you enjoy being a teacher, there is nothing wrong with telling the students that you are there because you enjoy teaching. Being cheerful, open, and understanding is always an asset to good teaching. Students will like to hear your experiential anecdotes — share them. Look upon the class as a project. Adult students expect planning and preparation and will not rebel if they are held to higher standards. Be aware of your cultural and intellectual environment. Strive to be a good and successful instructor and your teaching experiences will be exciting, rewarding, and satisfying.

 Take a few moments before your first class to meditate about your reasons for teaching. This will do two things: it will encourage you to more clearly identify your personal goals and it will increase your confidence.

There may be students who question why someone with your expertise would spend time teaching a college course. Be prepared. Have a few answers ready if students ask. If they don't ask, you might want to include it in your personal introduction. You certainly have good reasons. It might be to your advantage to communicate them. You may just enjoy teaching, like interaction with others, like the stimulation, enjoy being in front of a group, or feel it improves your own skills.

You should also give thought to your role in your institution. In short "what is an adjunct/part-time instructor?" Too often adjunct faculty, and thus their students, feel their place within the institution is temporary and unimportant. Nothing could be farther from the truth. Over the past decade, adjunct faculty have assumed a greater responsibility to the educational mission of their colleges and universities. Many institutions depend upon adjunct faculty for 50 percent or more of credit hours of instruction taught. Also in many institutions, adjunct and part-time faculty serve on committees and accept other non-instructional assignments. Finally, adjunct faculty often teach in specialized areas where specific qualifications and expertise is needed, such as marketing, management, accounting and entrepreneurship. Yes, whether you are a continuing adjunct or a last-minute hire, your role is important and necessary to the integrity and success of your institution.

 As with their full-time colleagues, teaching is still a vocation for many adjunct instructors, a calling to those individuals who enjoy being with people and feel an intrinsic satisfaction in helping others to grow.

In your role as an instructor, you will realize many of the intrinsic rewards of the profession. You are repaying your profession for its contributions to your own personal and professional development. There is satisfaction in providing service to your community. Teaching builds self esteem, offers personal rewards, and keeps you intellectually alive. Teaching can provide intellectual growth, community recognition and respect, and the development of new professional contacts. The satisfactions and rewards of being a good adjunct instructor are real and many.

What Business Students Need

All business students need knowledge "to go." They need concrete and well-presented information. Business students want to advance in their careers or jump to new career paths. Students presented with business theories need to understand how those theories translate into practice in the workplace. As your students read through the textbook and other assigned materials, they may not relate to the concepts or understand the true meaning of business theories until they interact with them in class discussions and through written assignments.

For business students, class discussions are particularly important, because the two-way communication allows students to present their viewpoints while learning about the perspectives and experiences of other students. This, in many ways, is the definition of business. Classroom discussions offer students the ability to ask questions, seek clarification, and receive guidance. Written assignments provide a less immediate form of two-way communication, and allow instructors to follow the logical development of students' thought processes in order to tailor feedback that is corrective and supportive.

Students taking entry-level business classes often think in terms of "need to" and "should" statements. These students often have a rigid attitude about the business world, believing that all organizations follow a standard set of operating procedures, and that organizational issues are easily identified and corrected through the implementation of business theories. Business instructors need to guide students through the process of critical analysis and the development of well-informed and researched perspectives. A learning environment which emphasizes critical thinking and analysis and builds communication, writing and research skills helps students meet their academic and career needs.

Business Basics

Business students often elect foundational courses to meet degree requirements. A student in a marketing class may have no interest in a marketing or sales-related position and believe that what s/he learns will not benefit a career in business. Through class lectures, written assignments and discussions, students learn that marketing skills, which include advertising and personal selling, have direct relevance to job functions for many business positions and are especially important for small business owners. Marketing skills also translate to writing a resume. Marketing one's self as the best candidate for a position involves selling skills and abilities to prospective employers. As an instructor, you have an opportunity to help students discover the importance of the course topics and how they relate to the business world.

Case Studies

The inclusion of a case study, either within the class discussions or as a basis for a written assignment, allows students to take textbook theories and translate them into real-world applications. You can use formal case studies which have been published in scholarly journals, or find real-world examples in current business publications. Your class could study a successful business then discuss and analyze the reasons for the company's success. You could also select and analyze a successful business leader in a business management class. Why not develop a hypothetical case study based on your business experience and background? The purpose of a case study is to promote the use of cognitive processing while expanding your students' understanding of the business world.

Research Methodologies

All students benefit from understanding the formalized process of research, which is often referred to as the scientific method of research. This teaches students to use logic and reasoning as they assess current business conditions, problems, situations or issues. Students also learn to separate facts from opinions, make statements that utilize critical analysis skills and write responses which are supported by credible sources.

As a general overview, the scientific method of research establishes a structure where issues and broad topics are first developed into concise research problem statements. Next, a background analysis or literature review is conducted as a means of establishing a gap or need for a new research study. Once a research problem has been identified and the need for a study solidified, a research design is developed. The research may be quantitative, qualitative or a mixed methods design.

Quantitative research utilizes numerical based data and qualitative research analyzes elements such as words, thoughts, and feelings. Each research design has specific methods to choose from. For example, a qualitative research design may utilize ethnography-based research, a case study or grounded theory methodology. After the research design has been clearly established the next step in the process is to collect data and then analyze it. After the data analysis is completed, conclusions related to the research problem statement are developed. A typical reaction from students is that they do not plan on conducting formalized research and do not see the value in learning about this process. In conducting their own research, students learn to examine issues closely, look for supporting facts and develop critical thinking skills.

Field Trips and Guest Lecturers

Field trips bring business students into real world environments to explore aspects of the business world from a hands-on perspective. For an adjunct instructor teaching a class on campus which meets only once a week, the idea of a field trip may not seem possible or logical, however, it is possible to develop an adapted form to enhance the process of learning. For instance, ask students to visit an organization or small business, talk to managers, leaders, or business owners as a means of gaining real-world perspectives to share with the class. Virtual field trips are an excellent alternative for adjunct business instructors who face time constraints which make regular field trips difficult. Students can visit websites, gather information, and contact organizations requesting information.

Another excellent option is to bring the organization or business to the classroom. Invite a guest speaker to address the class. This reinforces your lectures , the course concepts and brings the materials to life. Students should be allowed time to ask questions and interact with the speaker.

Establishing a Teaching Environment

Over the past decades, there has been a major movement in higher education called "the learning college" movement or community-centered learning. Quite simply, this means that learning has become student-centered rather than instructor-centered. This is especially important to adjunct faculty members, most of whom come from the surrounding business community and thus are aware of community mores.

When establishing a student-centered learning environment, one should first examine the teacher-student relationship. The simple and most obvious way to develop a relationship with your students is to be yourself and be honest. Establish communication in the classroom the same way you would in any other human endeavor. There are, however, additional specific steps that can be taken to establish a proper learning environment. Helen Burnstad describes four areas in which the learning environment should be examined: teacher expectations, teaching behavior, physical space, and strategies for creating an environment for learning (Burnstad, 2000). Although it is impossible to describe these areas completely in this handbook, some of Burnstad's major points are examined below:

- Teacher expectations. It is important that each instructor have a clear picture of his or her own style and expectations. The expectations that you as an instructor have of yourself may differ considerably from those of the students in your class. This does not mean that you need to change your style. However, you need to examine the expectations of your students in terms of their positions (rather than your position) on issues and principles that may arise in class. Also it is important that you consider your own teaching goals. From this you can frame your philosophy and intent regarding the content of the course.

- Teacher behaviors. It is important that you examine your presence in the classroom. Students will sense whether you really love your subject matter or are teaching the course to reach some unrelated professional goal. A pleasant personality is important. Enthusiasm may be demonstrated through energy and engaging in activities with students. Remember, your feelings concerning the expectations of your students will unwittingly be reflected in the success or failure of your students.

- Physical space. Although in most cases you will have little control over the physical aspects of the classroom environment, there are several things that can be done by the instructor. If possible, you may physically move seats so that dialogue and eye contact are easier. You should monitor the attention span of your students; sense the need for reinforcement; calculate the time-on-task; and encourage students to move, interact and ask questions.

- Environmental strategies. Some strategies that can improve the classroom environment include:

  1. **Introducing yourself** to your students with some personal anecdotes.

  2. **Being prepared** for students with diverse backgrounds.

  3. **Using an activity for getting to know** your students, whether a game, a writing assignment, or reference card, etc.

  4. **Learning each student's name** and providing ways for students to get to know one another.

  5. **Preparing a complete and lively syllabus**. You can have your students from a previous class leave a legacy by asking them to write a letter for incoming students then sharing it.

  6. **Using classroom assessment** techniques.

Finally, whether one is establishing a classroom environment or doing day-to-day activities, it is important that you be as positive in your student-teacher relationships as toward your subject matter. Make yourself available for student contact, either personally or electronically. Take a personal interest in each student and never judge or stereotype students.

Teaching Business: What It's All About

Characteristics of Good Teaching

Using one's mind in the pursuit of knowledge and at the same time sharing it with others is very gratifying. The responsibility for a class and the potential influence on students can be very stimulating. It remains stimulating, however, only so long as the instructor continues to grow and remains dynamic.

The qualities of good teaching are quite simple:

- Know your subject content.
- Know and like your students.
- Understand our culture.
- Possess professional teaching skills and strategies.

Knowing your subject means simply that you have a command of your discipline and the capability of calling upon resources. Knowing students is part of the teaching process and is aided by formal and informal communication within and outside the classroom. Understanding our cultural milieu has become increasingly complex for today's instructor. Sensitivity to the diverse cultures in your classroom is necessary to succeed in teaching. Finally, it is necessary that you continue to develop and improve strategies and techniques for the delivery of instruction in the classroom.

Some characteristics that students look for in good teachers are:

- Being knowledgeable, organized, and in control.
- Getting students actively involved in their learning.
- Helping students understand the course objectives and goals.
- Being a facilitator, not a director.

- Knowing the latest trends and technology.

- Stimulating discussion utilizing ice breakers.

- Preparing professional materials and handouts.

Setting the Tone

Education professionals and teacher trainers agree that creating positive feelings about the course is an important goal for any instructor. Often instructors assume that students know they intend to be pleasant, cooperative, and helpful. However, this should not be taken for granted. With differing personalities and types of students in the classroom, faculty members must realize that a positive comment or gesture to one student may in fact be negative to another student. Thus, you should make a concerted effort to be friendly. A smile, a pleasant comment, or a laugh with students who are attempting to be funny will pay great dividends.

In setting the tone of the classroom, permissiveness is sometimes a good strategy. We are all familiar with the old classroom where students were essentially "passive" learners. We are also familiar with situations where excessive permissiveness became a distraction to other students. Teachers of adults must realize that flexibility and permissiveness are important to a proper learning environment and that encouraging creativity and unexpected comments is part of the learning and teaching process. The instructor has ultimate authority so excessive distraction should always be controlled, but do not exercise authority for its own sake. Remember, permissiveness and flexibility requires considerable skill to work. Authority comes with the title of instructor.

Teachers as Actors and Actresses

In reality, teachers are on stage; they are actors or actresses whether or not they recognize and admit it. A teacher in front of the classroom carries all of the responsibility for the success of the performance, and this requires all of the talents of anyone on the stage. Due to modern technology, unfortunately, students compare faculty to professionals they have seen in other roles.

Thus, adjunct faculty must be alert to the ramifications of poor presentation. Faculty members have within themselves all of the emotions of stage performers but with greater audience interaction. There may occasionally be an emotional reaction in class and you should prepare for it. As an instructor, you will experience fear, joy and feelings of tentativeness and also feelings of extreme confidence and satisfaction. Handle fear with good preparation; confidence brought forward with good preparation is the easiest way to lessen fear. Remove anxieties from the classroom by developing communication systems. Some adjunct faculty members are effective at using humor.

 As a general rule, however, humor should be used delicately. Jokes are completely out. Almost any joke that is told will offend someone.

Classroom Communication

Many kinds of communication exist in every classroom situation. You must be aware that facial expressions and eye contact with students, as well as student interactions, are all forms of communication. It is your responsibility to ensure that classroom communication is structured in a positive manner. Communication starts the moment you enter the classroom for the first class session. The communication methods you use during the first class and the initial interaction with students are indicative of the types of communication that will exist throughout the course.

The amount of student participation as the course progresses is an indicator of the direction in which the communication is flowing; more is always better. Since many students today are adults, there is greater opportunity to call upon their experiences. The discussion of facts, events, examples, analogies, and anecdotes will often elicit an association for your adult students. This will encourage students to share experiences and anecdotes of their own.

Getting Down To Business

Do not assume that classroom communication can only be between the instructor and students. Communication in the classroom can take any number of forms. It can mean a room full of small group activities where students are discussing and interacting with each other as the instructor stands by silently. It can also include animated and serious discussions and even disagreements while addressing a specific problem or issue presented in class. One of your major responsibilities is to provide an instructor-directed setting in which students can communicate freely and maintain positive, goal-oriented communication.

Some specific instructor-led communication activities include the use of open-ended questions, critical thinking techniques, anecdotes, and problem-solving activities. Communication activities between students include buzz groups, a partner system, student panels, collaborative learning activities, student group reports, brainstorming and group discussions. Remember, a good class is dynamic, participative and interactive.

The Three R's of Teaching

Everyone remembers the three R's of learning. For any instructor, however, the three R's of teaching, are equally important. The three R's of good teaching are: **repeat**, **respond**, and **reinforce**. Very simply, student comments and contributions, if worthy of being recognized in class, are worthy of being repeated. A simple repeat, however, is not sufficient. You should elicit an additional response either from the class or the student making the original statement. After the response, you should offer a reinforcement of the statement or add your own conclusions. These three simple rules improve class relationships by emphasizing the importance of student contributions, relationships between students and the instructor's respect for all the students. This promotes two-way communication and represents the application of one of the basic tenets of learning—reinforcement.

Teaching Styles

Just as students have styles of learning, faculty have their own styles of teaching. Whether your style is one of planned preparation or a natural development, your style is important. For example, an instructor who emphasizes facts in teaching will have difficulty developing meaningful discussions with students who have progressed to the analysis stage of their learning. It is not important that part-time instructors modify their behavior to match that of students. It is important, however, that part-time faculty recognize their own teaching styles and adapt teaching processes, techniques and strategies to enhance their most effective style. Some questions to assist you in determing your teaching style are:

- Do I tend to be authoritative, directional, semi-directional or laissez-faire in my classroom leadership?
- Do I solicit communication with and between students easily or with difficulty?
- Am I well-organized and prepared?
- Am I meticulous in my professional appearance or do I have a tendency to put other priorities first and show up in class as is?

 A common mistake for many instructors is that they assume their students will learn in the same manner in which the instructor learned as a student.

Therefore, it would be wise to examine some of the basic learning styles of students, discussed in detail in Chapter 2. By understanding student learning styles, you can modify your teaching techniques to be certain that your presentation style does not turn off certain students.

For example, if you tended to learn best from a direct no-

nonsense instructor, then chances are you will lean toward that type of behavior in your own teaching. This would satisfy students who learn in that manner; however, there will be students in your class who are more successful in a more laissez-faire environment that gives more freedom of expression. If you thrive on open communication and discussion in your learning process, expecting this from all of your students may be a false hope since many students are silent learners and may be intimidated by the need to verbally participate in class.

These are only a few examples of the types of teaching style adjustments that may be necessary to become an effective facilitator of learning. I have found that teaching styles are not static. Many of the techniques I used early in my career with younger students who appreciated humor and diversion were not as effective later with more mature students who felt they were there to learn, not to be entertained. I also noticed later in my career that although I was well-organized, had well-stated objectives, used good class communication, and observed the characteristics that I deemed important to good teaching, I had become too serious. For that reason I now occasionally mix in with my lesson plan an additional sheet that says to me, "smile, be friendly, smell the roses."

Also, I have found an evolution in the use of anecdotes. Strangely enough it was the reverse. Early in my career the use of anecdotes sometimes drew criticism from students as "too much story telling," or "more war stories." Later I began to put the question on my evaluation questionnaires: "Were the anecdotes and stories meaningful?" The overwhelming response from adult students was "yes." They were pertinent, they brought meaning to the class, and they were valuable because the adults were interested in real life experiences rather than rote lecturing.

 One note of caution, however, the use of anecdotes should relate to the topic being discussed and not simply stories of other experiences.

In general, most students will approve of anecdotes and may have their own to contribute. Always be ready for students to share.

If you wish to do a quick analysis of your style, it can easily be done using the Internet. One such survey is "Gardner's Multiple Intelligences," available on most major search engines. This survey allows you to examine your strengths in eight categories, allowing you to analyze your own strengths and weaknesses in relation to your students. Although you need to be aware of copyright restrictions, many sites have surveys available with copyright permission granted so you can even use them in class.

A meaningful exercise might be to have your students complete the survey on their own (it is non-threatening) and discuss the composite results and what they mean in class.

Professional Ethics

Although the teaching profession has been slow (compared to other professions) to address ethical issues, developments of the past few decades has encouraged an examination of the ethical status of college faculty. Although the recent attention has been inspired by legal or public relations concerns, there has always existed an unwritten code of ethics for teachers based upon values that have evolved both within the teaching profession and our culture.

Dr. Wilbert McKeachie states, "Ethical standards are intended to guide us in carrying out the responsibilities we have to the different groups with whom we interact" (McKeachie, 1994).

Some institutions have adopted written standards of ethical behavior expected of all college faculty. A compilation of some of these standards is listed below as an example and all adjunct/

part-time faculty should check with their department director or dean for information on their institution's standards. For clarity, the guidelines are presented in two categories: those pertaining to the profession of teaching and those pertaining to students.

Check with your institution to see if there is a college-wide code of ethics for faculty members and/or students. Review your institution's standards carefully, and clarify those expectations with your department chair, director or dean. A compilation of some of these standards is listed below:

Ethics and The Business Instructor

While these guidelines are general in nature, they provide a vehicle for examining the ethical expectations of the institution where you teach. These guidelines will also ensure that you have a strong academic reputation. You serve as a representative of your institution and your classroom behavior and performance become the institution in your students' eyes. Another growing area of professional ethics is the use of social networking websites and many institutions are beginning to address this issue with their ethics policies. The best rule of thumb is to connect with colleagues only through professional websites and avoid personal contacts or connections with your students through social networking websites.

Ethics and the Profession

This section is an attempt to emphasize the ethical expectations of the profession and the institution in which part-time faculty are employed.

Adjunct faculty:

- Will attend all assigned classes with adequately prepared materials and content as described in the course description.
- Will not attempt to teach a course for which they are not qualified and knowledgeable.
- Will present all sides on controversial issues.
- Will conduct a fair evaluation of students, applied equally to all.

- Will not promote outside entrepreneurial activities within the class setting.

- When reasonably possible, will attend college orientations and other development activities presented for the improvement of their role as an instructor.

- Will avoid behavior that may be interpreted as discriminatory based upon gender, age, social status or racial background.

- Will hold their colleagues and institution in highest respect in their actions and communication within and outside the institution.

Professional Ethics and Students

This section relates to ethical considerations concerning students.

Adjunct faculty:

- Won't discuss students and their problems outside of the professional structure of the institution.

- Will refer student personal problems to qualified staff.

- Will maintain and honor office hours and appointments with students.

- Will respect students' integrity and avoid social encounters with students which might suggest misuse of power.

- Will not attempt to influence students' philosophy or their positions concerning social and political issues.

- Will not ask students for personal information for research purposes.

These guidelines are quite general; however, they provide a vehicle for examining more closely the expectations of the institution in which you teach. Unfortunately, in today's world, there is sometimes a fine line between ethical issues and legal issues.

More formal statements of professional standards are available from the American Association of University Professors, "Statement on Professional Ethics," adopted in 2009, <http://www.aaup.org/AAUP/pubres/policydocs/contents/statementonprofessionalethics.htm>, as well as the National Education Association.

For purposes of brevity, only the NEA's "Commitment to the Student" under the Code of Ethics of the Education Profession is presented here. <http://www.nea.org/home/30442.htm>

The educator strives to help each student realize his or her potential as a worthy and effective member of society. The educator therefore works to stimulate the spirit of inquiry, the acquisition of knowledge and understanding, and the thoughtful formulation of worthy goals.

In fulfillment of the obligation to the student, the educator—
- Shall not unreasonably restrain the student from independent action in the pursuit of learning.
- Shall not unreasonably deny the student's access to varying points of view.
- Shall not deliberately suppress or distort subject matter relevant to the student's progress.
- Shall make reasonable effort to protect the student from conditions harmful to learning or to health and safety.
- Shall not intentionally expose the student to embarrassment or disparagement.
- Shall not on the basis of race, color, creed, sex, national origin, marital status, political or religious beliefs, family, social or cultural background, or sexual orientation, unfairly:
  a. exclude any student from participation in any program.
  b. deny benefits to any student.
  c. grant any advantage to any student.

- Shall not use professional relationships with students for private advantage.
- Shall not disclose information about students obtained in the course of professional service unless disclosure serves a compelling professional purpose or is required by law (NEA, 1975).

Academic Dishonesty

Academic dishonesty usually appears in two forms: outright cheating or plagiarism. The problem of cheating in college classrooms has probably become more common in the last few years due to the pressures on students to succeed. Adding to the problem is the fact that we offer student instruction in conducting research online, which in turn leads to temptation to copy and paste materials found online rather than to conduct original research.

To minimize cheating, some instructors place a significant percentage of the student evaluation in the form of shared or active student participation. These activities are evaluated for all members of the group, thus providing no incentive for individuals to attempt to cheat to better themselves. It is important also that in the classroom environment ethical responsibilities requiring trust and honesty are emphasized. The traditional method of countering cheating is to develop multiple tests with different questions and to not repeat the same test or test questions term after term.

Regardless of the amount of trust built in a classroom situation, all exams should be proctored and you should never leave the room in which an exam is being conducted. The instructor is ethically responsible for this commitment to the students who are striving honestly to achieve their goals and make their grade and to the institution. Extra time spent by the instructor to devise an evaluation plan in which written tests are only part of the final grade is time well spent. On the final exam, students may be asked to write in their own words the two or three principles that affected them most in the course and what they feel they may gain in the future. This question could represent a significant part of the final grade.

Getting Down To Business

If you suspect or encounter a student in the act of cheating or plagiarism, the student should be made aware of the situation. This should be done in confidence in a face-to-face meeting.

 In the legalistic world we live in, there can only be one conclusive bit of advice: as an instructor, you must be aware of your institution's official procedures and the legal status of your position.

Suspecting someone of cheating or actually seeing is an unpleasant experience; however, it will likely happen in your teaching experience sooner or later. Usually, reasonable rational procedures will adequately cover the situation without the destruction of the student's academic career or standing.

To learn more about academic dishonesty and how to deal with it, refer to the ERIC Digest "It Takes a Village: Academic Dishonesty & Educational Opportunity," published in 2005, **<http://www.eric.ed.gov/ERICWebPortal/detail?accno=EJ720381>**

In addition, you may want to visit the web site of the Center for Academic Integrity at **<http://www.academicintegrity.org>**.

Checklist for Part-Time Faculty

There are many things that you need to know when receiving your teaching assignment. Each teaching situation may call for new information. There are, however, basic items that will almost assuredly be asked sometime during class. This section lists information you may wish to check before entering the first class.

(After reviewing this list, it is recommended that a personal timeline be developed including these and other important dates related to teaching the course.)

Figure 1.1—Faculty Checklist

1. What are the names of the department chairperson, dean, director and other important officials?

2. Have I completed all of my paperwork for official employment? (It's demoralizing when an expected paycheck doesn't arrive.)

3. Is there a pre-term faculty meeting? Date_____
   Time_____

4. Is there a departmental course syllabus, course outline, or statement of goals and objectives available for the course?

5. Are there prepared departmental handouts?

6. Are there prepared departmental tests?

7. Where is and/or how do I get my copy of the text(s) and support materials for teaching the class?

8. Is there a department and/or college attendance or tardiness policy?

9. When are grades due? When do students receive grades?

10. Is there a college or departmental grading policy?

11. Where can I get instructional aid materials and equipment, films, CD/DVDs, software? What is the lead time for ordering?

12. How do I get a college email account set-up?

13. Does the college offer course web site templates?

14. Who are some of the other faculty who have taught the course? Are they open to assisting adjuncts?

15. Where can I find information to develop a list of resources and references pertaining to outside student assignments?

16. Have the course objectives been reviewed to be certain they reflect changes in text materials or technology?

17. Do I have a variety of instructional strategies planned so that my course does not become repetitious?

18. Do I have a current academic calendar that lists the length of term, the end of quarter, semester, or inter-term for special assignment so everyone clearly understands the beginning and termination of the course?

CHAPTER 2
ALL ABOUT ADULT STUDENTS

Why Trust Matters

On the first day of class, students may choose to trust the instructor, or students may withhold judgment. Trust is based on how the students perceive an instructor's ability to facilitate the class. Instructors can encourage student trust through positive interactions, meaningful conversations and the establishment of conditions which promote productive working relationships.

What does it mean for students to trust their instructors? If students have developed a sense of trust, they will rely upon the instructor's experience and background. They trust that the instructor will effectively facilitate class discussions, provide meaningful feedback and assist them in meeting the learning objectives. Students expect instructors to bring the course materials to life in a way that they can understand, relate to and apply in the real world.

Students are receptive to instructors whom they trust and with whom they can communicate, rather than instructors who simply make demands. An instructor can request or expect that students will be involved in the class; however, students will devote their fullest time and effort to the process of learning when they feel a connection to the class and to the instructor—you!

It takes time and care to develop a trusting relationship. Every interaction and every form of communication between the instructor and her/his students needs to build pathways to trust. Monitor the tone of your communications, whether verbal or electronic. Preparation, attitude, availability and responsiveness to students' needs all help establish trust.

It may not be possible to gauge the exact level of trust that develops over time, but every interaction produces a perceptual result. Each positive interaction is another step in the right direction on your path toward establishing the trust needed to work effectively with your students.

Meeting Students' Needs

Your students are self-directed by nature, which means they want to participate in the process of learning and have choices about their level of involvement. Students get involved during class discussions in which they are asked to share their ideas, experience and knowledge. Class discussions also provide you with an opportunity to add relevance to the course. Instructors can connect students to the course topics by sharing real world examples, the instructors' own experience and supplemental resources—materials which bring the course materials to life.

Students should be given choices about assignment topics so that learning is relevant. Students are motivated when they believe they can complete the assigned tasks or participate in class discussions in meaningful ways, and the information acquired will lead to the creation of knowledge that is relevant to their personal and professional lives. While it's not possible to create excitement and enthusiasm for every class activity and assignment, it is important to make sure activities are not "busy work" but rather relevant to the learning objectives.

Getting Students Engaged in the Process of Learning

Engagement is defined as the energy and effort a student devotes to his or her class. The process of being engaged in the class involves more than the student just "getting by" or doing the minimum required to pass the course. When a student is engaged in the class, that student devotes the time necessary to become an active participant in the process of learning. The student's attention is focused in and out of class on the course materials. Engaged students are highly-involved in the class, which in turn leads to improved performance.

Getting Down To Business

Active engagement leads to increased participation in class discussions — often an excellent gauge of a student's motivation. Remember that the level of student engagement will frequently change, depending upon the course materials, interactions and experiences with other students and the instructor. If students are feeling confident with their progress in a class, that will enhance their engagement.

Instructors influence student engagement by providing support and guidance, being dynamic, developing meaningful interactions and demonstrating engagement through their participation, passion and enthusiasm. Students who see their instructor as present in their class will be more active and engaged in the class, as well. It's important to establish conditions that help students stay motivated. A strong working relationship, one that provides support and guidance, is the most effective tool for student motivation. The goal is to create a professional, open learning environment.

The process of adult learning involves more than giving students the course materials, creating assignments and providing feedback. Your students have academic and professional needs. They will acquire knowledge and skills to meet those needs in your classroom. Adult learning principles explain how these processes occur, and while theory alone will not address every situation or guarantee effective facilitation, knowledge of these basic principles will provide insight necessary to develop tools and techniques to address students' pedagogical needs.

Once you have read through the adult learning theories that are presented in this chapter and you have a better understanding of these learning processes, you'll be able to put that knowledge to work for you. For example, when you are assigned to teach a course, there may not be the flexibility to select the textbook or create the syllabus. What you *can* control, however, is your approach to teaching those materials.

The first two principles, andragogy and self-directed learning, remind instructors that adults want to be actively involved in the process of learning. Adult students make choices about their level of involvement and participation in the class. The theory of transformational learning describes the role of cognitive development in the process of adult education. All of the adult learning principles reviewed in this chapter recognize the unique nature of an adult's developmental needs. The co-creative process of adult learning is directly influenced by interactions with the instructor, other students and the overall classroom or learning environment.

Andragogy: The Essence of an Adult Learner

If you are the typical part-time instructor today, you were probably first introduced to teaching using the methods of pedagogy. Pedagogy is based upon the teaching of children and is synonymous with the word "leader" (Knowles, 1990). In the past several years, however, the role of the teacher has changed from being a leader or presenter of learning to being a facilitator of learning because the average age of the college student today is closer to 30 than to the 20 years old of a few years ago. This older and more diverse student body will come to class motivated to learn but with a different set of needs. They are likely goal-oriented problem solvers and bring with them a need to know why they are learning something.

Thus came the acceptance of the andragogical model pioneered by Knowles. The andragogical model is based upon:

- The student's need to know
- The learner's self concept
- The role of the learner's experience
- The readiness to learn
- An orientation to learning
- Motivation.

Getting Down To Business

Andragogy has often been called the art and science of teaching adults because it places the student at the center of the learning process and emphasizes collaborative relationships among students and with the instructor—all techniques that work well with adult students. The andragogical model prescribes problem solving activities based upon the students' needs rather than on the goals of the discipline or the instructor.

Developing an andragogical teaching strategy requires a warm and friendly classroom environment to foster open communication. You must be aware that many adults have anxieties about their learning experience and lack confidence. Thus, plan activities that make students feel confident and secure with opportunities for students to share their experiences. It is important that this classroom environment be cultivated and nurtured in the first class session and that you establish yourself as a partner in learning and not an expert who has all the answers.

To incorporate the techniques of andragogy in your class, it is necessary that you become proficient in executing student-centered activities including: conducting a meaningful discussion, stimulating cooperative learning, developing good questions and critical thinking strategies, and involving all students in the learning process.

Student Learning Styles

One can easily find many paradigms for student learning styles in educational literature. Faculty are not expected to master or study in detail all of these styles and then attempt to categorize their students. It is, however, useful for you to understand some of the different learning styles that may appear in your classroom so that you can give consideration to individual differences. One such learning style system is called the "4mat system." This system identifies four types of learners. They are: **imaginative learners**, **analytic learners**, **common sense learners** and **dynamic learners**.

- **Imaginative learners** will expect the faculty member to produce authentic curricula, to present knowledge upon which to build, to involve them in group work, and to provide useful feedback. They care about fellow students and the instructor.

- **Analytic learners** are more interested in theory and what the experts think, they need details and data, and are uncomfortable with subjectiveness. They expect the class to enhance their knowledge and place factual knowledge over creativity.
- **Common sense learners** test theories and look for practical applications; they are problem solvers and are typically skill oriented. They expect to be taught skills and may not be flexible or good in teamwork situations.
- **Dynamic learners** believe in self-discovery. They like change and flexibility, are risk takers, and are at ease with people. They may, however, be pushy and manipulative. They respond to dynamic instructors who are constantly trying new things (McCarthy, 1987).

It is important to understand that all or some of these types of learners may be present in any given class. This makes it necessary for the instructor to possess the ability to use a variety of classroom activities.

I recall an experience while teaching that relates to this topic. Having for years been successful in teaching classes by encouraging open communication and maximizing student involvement, I found myself teaching a class in which an acquaintance was enrolled. This person simply would not respond or take part in discussions. Knowing the student to be social and bright, I was not completely surprised that when all the criteria for grades were considered, the individual easily earned an "A," contrary to my belief that all students must participate to learn! It was only later that I realized that the student process for learning was not flawed, it was just different from the style that I, as the instructor, had perceived necessary for learning.

Closely reviewing the description of student types will bring out another important factor. That is, just as students have learning styles, teachers have teaching styles. Thus, you should be able to identify your own teaching style from the learning style descriptions. Understanding your teaching style will allow you to modify your behavior to accommodate all learners.

After considering the learning styles above, it is just as important to keep in mind two major factors concerning adult learners. First, they have basically been trained to be cognitive learners so they will first seek to obtain the knowledge and information that they feel is necessary to complete the course work and receive a passing grade. Second, adults learn by doing. They want to take part in learning activities based upon their needs and application. When interacting with individual students in your classroom, you must continually recognize that all learners are not coming from the same set of circumstances.

Assessing Learning Styles

There are four primary theories or measures of adult learning styles. Instructors should always remember that a one-size-fits-all approach to education is not effective. Your adult students will not only gravitate toward a primary approach to learning, they may use a combination of one or more learning styles. The following assessment tools help students and instructors identify elements related to the process of adult learning:

1. **The Myers Briggs Type Indicator** utilizes a set of questions that focus on perceptions and the results produce one of sixteen possible personality types. This measurement can relate students' personality characteristics to the process of learning from a perceptual perspective.

2. **VARK** is based upon the senses and is comprised of Visual (seeing), Aural (hearing), Read/Write, and Kinesthetic (bodily/physical).

3. **The Multiple Intelligences** inventory was developed by Dr. Howard Gardner and provides a list of eight types of learning styles, including verbal, musical, logical, inter-personal, visual, intra-personal, bodily and naturalistic.

4. **The Kolb Learning Style Inventory** is based upon a circular process of learning that considers the students' experiences, reflections, thoughts, and actions. Kolb's theory developed four learning styles that are based upon various combinations of the following components of the learning cycle: feeling, thinking, watching and doing.

Knowledge of adult learning styles provides numerous benefits to classroom instructors. A course is typically developed to create specific learning outcomes in order to meet accreditation guidelines and standards. Activities are then designed to help students meet the expected course outcomes. This means that the curriculum designer may not include activities which address every learning style. Instructors can address the needs of various learning styles in their lectures, presentations and facilitation strategies. For example, by understanding that adult students interact with information and process it in a variety of ways, instructors can add interactive elements, such as audio and video, to their class presentations and lectures. In addition, instructors can identify their own personal learning style and recognize how that impacts the way they teach.

Self-Directed (Student-Centered) Learning

Self-directed or student-centered learning builds upon the premise of andragogy. It does not indicate the absence of an instructor's guidance or assistance. Instead, it suggests adult students understand the overall purpose of obtaining a formal education and more importantly, that they are willing to take responsibility for their own role in the process. The instructor provides the tools and support necessary to do so, such as offering options for self-directed learning activities and independent study projects.

 While there may not be a lot of flexibility in the curriculum—particularly if following a departmental syllabus— the business instructor can still find methods of offering choices.

Getting Down To Business

For example, instructors can provide a list of topics, case studies or problems for students to choose from when completing a written assignment. This would not change the curriculum or the pre-developed learning activities established for the course, and could actually enhance it if the instructor were provided with the flexibility to add such enhancements.

Student-centered instructional strategies help to create a collaborative learning environment. When students are given choices, they are provided with the flexibility necessary to become self-directed and co-creators in the learning process. A student-centered approach also requires that instructors take into account the perspective of their students, and include real-world scenarios and examples to add relevance to the class. Instructors should encourage students to apply what they have learned. It is important to note that self-directed learning does not mean students become independent learners who do not need a structured learning environment. Adult students rely upon their instructors for guidance in the development of skill sets, assistance with processing information, knowledge of theory as applied to the real world and meaningful classroom experience as a teacher and business professional.

Acquisition and Creation of Knowledge

One of the main purposes of adult education programs is to establish classroom conditions necessary for learning to take place. In successful learning environments, information is presented through course materials and resources, classroom lectures, online postings, discussions and student research. Adult learning involves the acquisition of information, interaction with that information through assigned activities and the creation of new knowledge.

Adults acquire knowledge through informal and formal processes. Informal learning occurs through everyday activities and experiences—by trial and error. An adult may also acquire knowledge while performing job-related tasks. Knowledge comes from critical thinking, logic and reasoning. When adults seek specialized knowledge that they believe they cannot acquire on their own, they may end up in your college classroom.

Formal learning is a structured process with objectives, goals and expected learning outcomes. You should develop learning objectives, checkpoints along the way, for each week of the course. Learning activities are then developed to allow students to demonstrate their progress, skill set development, and knowledge acquired. Adult students are seeking knowledge which is relevant to their lives and their particular needs. This is especially true of returning students—students who simultaneously work in a business field while pursing a degree. They will only work toward those objectives if they believe that the learning goals are aligned with their needs. It becomes crucial, then, for an instructor to acknowledge the students' need for relevant and meaningful knowledge by establishing activities which contribute to their learning. So-called "busy work" has no place in the college classroom. Student success is a function of classroom structure and instructor preparedness.

Adult students don't automatically "download" knowledge by entering the classroom, receiving information that has been presented in the course materials or even by completing the assignments. The most common forms of course information include textbook readings, literature and scholarly articles and supplemental materials provided by the instructor. This is referred to as explicit knowledge or information that has been written down or recorded. Students already possess a knowledge base, and this is the reference point that they access when evaluating new information received. This is tacit knowledge, knowledge based upon students' experiences, beliefs and/or perceptions.

The creation of new knowledge occurs in the classroom learning environment as a result of interactions with the instructor and other students. They exchange ideas, experiences and knowledge. As students take this information, process it and interact with it in a meaningful way they expand their knowledge base. This is why the instructor needs to include a wide variety of learning activities as part of the class so that students have different methods of interacting with information and multiple sources of information available to them.

Getting Down To Business

For instance, if students conduct research, but they are not provided with an opportunity to discuss how they are processing this information, they (and the instructor) will have lost a valuable opportunity for intellectual development. Why? Because the students will not have explored other perspectives and alternate viewpoints related to this new information—exploration enriches the adult learning experience. In the classroom, however, student-centered learning takes on a different meaning. Most contemporary institutions have adopted many educational delivery strategies to accommodate students in many ways in order to assist them in meeting their educational needs. In a learner-centered classroom, faculty are expected to implement strategies that allow students more self-determination in how they reach their goals. This objective is, however, tempered by the need of departments and disciplines to set explicit achievement standards that must be met to fulfill the goals of the academic discipline.

Some questions you may need to ask yourself to assess your goal of a student-centered learning environment are listed below.

- Do I have strategies to encourage **open communication** among students and between students and the teacher?
- Do I have appropriate **feedback mechanisms** in place so that the feelings and the needs of the students are communicated in a meaningful and timely manner?
- Do I have **collaborative learning strategies** in my lesson plans so students can work as teams, groups, or partners?
- Are the **needs of the students** being met along with the objectives of the course?
- Do I **recognize students as individuals** with diverse backgrounds and needs as well as classroom participants?
- Do I **vary my teaching strategies** to accommodate a wide range of students?

Remember, a student-centered environment does not diminish the responsibility of the teacher nor give the students the power to determine course activities. Rather a student-centered environment requires skillful knowledge and use of cooperative and student-involved strategies implemented by the teacher.

Adult Student Diversity

There are some specific teaching strategies regarding student diversity of which you should be aware. When contemplating the course content you should consider the age of the students and their experiences. For example, when older students contribute anecdotes, they usually use their own past experiences. While younger students may prefer topics that effect them immediately. In understanding student attitudes and behaviors, keep in mind that many older students were educated in structured classroom settings and are accustomed to formal lecture and discussion formats, while younger students will probably respond to a more active learning style. Older students also will have the confidence to share their experiences and backgrounds with the class whereas younger students may hesitate.

Above all avoid stereotyping any members of our culture. J. Solomon (1994) makes specific suggestions concerning diversity in the classroom. Some of his suggestions are:

- Learn to pronounce student names correctly. Avoid the use of nicknames.
- Do not tell or tolerate racist, sexist, ethnic or age-related jokes.
- Do not imply negatives when addressing other ethnic groups or culturally different societies.
- Become aware of your own prejudices.
- Never allow your own personal values to be the sole basis for judgment.
- Constantly evaluate your cultural perceptions to be sure they are not based upon personal insecurities.

Generally keep in mind that the diverse classroom provides several opportunities. Diversity provides an enriching experience when students share with each other and with the instructor, and may assist in reducing cultural barriers. The diverse class provides a forum for understanding the differences that exist between individuals and social classes. Through group interactive strategies, these differences can give students the chance to be full participants in their learning and development process. These group strategies can also provide opportunities for all students to become a part of their classroom community regardless of their background.

Cognitive Development and Bloom's Taxonomy

If there is a single paradigm that has stood the test of time in education it is Benjamin Bloom's *Taxonomy of Educational Objectives* (Bloom et al., 1956). Published more than half a century ago, this taxonomy describes the learning process as three factors or domains. They are the cognitive domain, affective domain and psychomotor domain.

Essentially, cognitive learning is learning that emphasizes knowledge and information and incorporates analysis of that knowledge. Affective learning centers on values and value systems, receiving stimuli, ideas and to some degree, organization. Psychomotor learning addresses hand/eye coordination, normally referred to as physical coordination.

The importance of these three domains is not so much the overall consideration of the categories as it is the breakdown provided by Bloom. For example, Bloom's cognitive domain is broken into several categories: knowledge, comprehension, application, analysis, synthesis and evaluation. The affective domain is broken into receiving, responding, valuing, organizing and characterization of value complex. A psychomotor domain essentially is that which provides for the development of physical skills.

The cognitive domain is usually emphasized in the classroom learning situation. However, when writing course objectives it is often expected that all three domains will be represented. This means that you should have objectives in the cognitive domain written not only at the knowledge level but also the evaluation, analysis and synthesis levels. In the affective domain, you would have objectives covering responding, valuing and value complex. Many institutions require course objectives and activities in all three of the domains of Bloom's Taxonomy. It should be noted from examination of the descriptions rendered here that these domains effectively cover all areas of the learning process.

The basic premise of cognition revolves around the way in which adult students retain knowledge and process information — how adult students learn. Bloom's Taxonomy is often cited for its explanation of the adults' cognitive functions, which includes the process of knowledge acquisition and the development of intellectual skills. Adults typically perform at lower level cognitive levels when dealing with everyday life experiences. These kinds of experiences utilize the cognitive processes of remembering and recalling information, as informal learning often does not require higher mental processing. The formal process of learning promotes higher-order cognitive development, which includes the following functions as described in Bloom's Taxonomy: application, analysis, synthesis and evaluation.

When students are presented with information in class, information that is often procedural and theoretical in nature, they are at first passive participants in the learning process. As the course progresses, students engage in learning activities. They will either be asked to work with their own knowledge base, report factual information or seek out new sources of information.

 If the learning activities do not require students to do anything more than recite or report knowledge, their cognitive abilities will remain at a lower level of functioning.

An example of a learning activity that utilizes only lower level cognitive functions includes a test or exam which asks students to memorize and recall facts and information. Higher-order cognition involves taking information and processing it in some way. This is interactive learning.

Getting Down To Business

Critical Thinking

Students also utilize higher-order cognitive skills when they use techniques which guide their thought processes or methods of thinking. Critical thinking provides the foundation necessary to guide students through the cognitive development process. Critical thinking encourages students to seek answers, find new solutions, consider alternatives, explore other options, develop their own ideas and solutions, and ask questions about what they have read or heard. When students work with information in a critically reflective manner not only are they moving to higher-order thinking and becoming active participants in the learning process, they also create new knowledge.

The ability to move from lower-level cognitive functioning to higher-level cognitive thinking requires time, experience and practice on the part of the adult student. It also requires careful planning, patience and instructional skill on the part of the faculty member. As an instructional strategy in the business classroom, the process of encouraging cognitive development can begin by adding current events, issues and challenges into the learning activities. This will prompt students to engage in higher-order thought processes. The inclusion of real-life examples, case studies, etc. supports discussions of the course materials. Students relate to that information through their personal and professional experiences, which in turn leads to intellectual development.

 Students taught to develop higher-order thinking skills learn to develop solutions and responses based upon logic and reasoning rather than beliefs and opinions.

Should instructors care what their students are thinking? Absolutely! Students are expected to be involved in the process of learning and to be focused on meeting the assigned learning objectives. They are required to have (or develop) the ability to rationally think through their assignments and discussions, while creating knowledge, gaining new perspectives and developing new skill sets. Students are challenged to look beyond their current belief systems, knowledge, opinions and ideas. This can be accomplished through the use of a formalized system of analysis known as critical thinking. Critical thinking is an internalized process of self-reflection, examination and questioning that causes a transition from lower-order thinking to higher-order thinking. Critical thinking involves the use of logic and reasoning, while separating facts from opinions. The process of learning is greatly enhanced when students develop and apply critical thinking. It promotes meaningful classroom exchanges and improved intellectual development.

When students begin to organize their thoughts they are using a logical thought process because it is a structured way of thinking. Students often accept what they believe as fact, especially if those "facts" are long-held beliefs. Critical thinking does more than simply ask students to consider what they think; it challenges them to consider *why* they believe what they believe. Critical thinking and reflection require continued practice. Students can examine beliefs, problems and issues through class discussions, role playing, real-world examples and written assignments. Critical thinking helps students develop a broader basis of diverse views by having an open mind and being receptive to other students' contributions, opinions, ideas and experiences.

Critical thinking skills do not always develop naturally. Students process information daily based upon their unique perspectives, which include their experience, skills, intelligence and existing knowledge. Students may experience something that prompts reflective thinking such as a job loss, a marriage or divorce, a new career or anything else that triggers an self-examination of their lives or recent events. While self-examination triggers reflection and introspection, it is the ability to think in a critically reflective manner that must be taught. Instructors can encourage the development of these skills by requiring students to analyze real-world situations, to develop new ideas, consider a variety of solutions and search for credible sources.

Getting Down To Business

 As students strive to reach higher cognitive levels, the ability to think critically becomes enhanced and their classroom performance improves. Why? Because your students are now actively engaged in the process of learning. Students benefit from the process of critical thinking by learning to make informed decisions and develop ideas that are supported by research. Students rely on logic and reasoning to evaluate assigned problems, search for answers to career-related issues, assess potential organizational solutions and weigh the credibility of sources obtained for their assignments.

Critical thinking is crucial to learning because students gather information and transform it by analyzing it. They acquire knowledge which meets the course objectives, as well as their developmental and professional needs. This process provides instructors with a very important means of measuring progress towards course outcomes and learning objectives.

Transformational Learning

Transformational learning focuses on the cognitive process of reflective thought as a means of learning. Transformation is an intellectual process which examines one's thoughts, feelings, belief systems and underlying assumptions. The intended outcome of transformative learning is a new awareness of self, development of new perspectives and the motivation to create personal change. The difference between the transformational learning theory and other adult education theories is that it considers the process of *how* the student develops what they know, rather than focusing on the knowledge they currently possess.

Adult students acquire knowledge and construct views informally through social interactions, written words and the media. Through formalized education students are likely to become aware of other views, opinions, beliefs and alternate ways of creating new knowledge. Transformational learning occurs when students discover new perspectives about the way they have created meaning for their lives. For the students, this process of retrospection and transformation begins in the classroom and continues as a process of lifelong learning.

When teaching adult students, the theory of transformational learning has the greatest potential for effectiveness when utilized as an instructional tool rather than as a method of curriculum design. Transformational learning may be approached as a planned process within the classroom, one that the instructor fully explains to students. It is important to consider that the process of transforming students' views and belief systems takes time, effort and planned guidance on the part of an instructor. Transformational learning does not offer quick results.

Instructors may ask students to reflect on their belief systems and then challenge them to consider alternate views through class discussions, self-assessments and group work. Class discussions provide students with opportunities to share diverse views and relate what they are experiencing and feeling. Another method of kicking off the transformational process in the business classroom is to ask students to solve a problem and collaborate in groups with consensus as the goal. This problem-solving method allows students to evaluate possible solutions and consider alternate ways of thinking. As students begin to consider other perspectives, they become personally transformed and the process of learning is enhanced. Transformative learning also requires students to make assessments of their existing belief system and determinations concerning the validity of their views. Students decide to accept their current beliefs, opinions and knowledge, or adopt new beliefs as a result of the process of exploration and discovery.

Defining Student Motivation

Student motivation is internalized and often manifested to the instructor through the student's overall performance and engagement in the class. Motivation is driven by internal and external needs, influenced by students' feelings, perceptions and attitudes about the learning process. When students are highly-motivated and active participants in the class, learning is enhanced. Conflict, lack of meaningful feedback or other negatives in the classroom can decrease self-motivation. When you understand how student motivation influences learning, you can implement motivational strategies and develop instructional techniques to interact with students in a meaningful way.

 Consider why some students appear to be highly-involved in the class and others may not. Motivational factors include personal and professional development, career advancement or change, educational requirements established by the students' employer, completion of a degree or certificate or the fulfillment of a lifelong goal.

Another way to understand your students' motivation is to consider a general theory about adult needs and how these needs drive internal self-motivation.

Internal and External Motivation

Maslow's Hierarchy of Needs explains the sense of internal motivation. A common internal motivator is your students' need for specific knowledge, which is directly related to their decision to pursue an educational program. Students' internal motivation may also be influenced by perceptions and expectations held about the learning process, along with their sense of identity, which can be formulated or shaped through classroom interactions.

External motivation is often the result of grades that students hope or expect to receive, along with the anticipated rewards expected for completing an assignment or their degree program. Motivation may also be the result of societal pressures which involve the student's career choice or career plans, family obligations or other lifestyle expectations. It is important to note that these external factors and expectations may or may not be realistic, which can create conflict when students experience the reality of being in school and completing their educational goals.

When students enter the class they are guided by their internal and external sources of motivation. Understanding these factors allows instructors to make learning relevant, which will help meet students' needs; however, there is much more for instructors to consider. Student motivation also includes self-motivation, which is required to maintain progress in the process of learning. While self-motivation is influenced by internal and external needs, it is also a product of interactions that occur throughout the class. Throughout this book, there are motivational strategies which an instructor can adopt to connect with students in a positive manner.

Maslow's Hierarchy of Needs in the Business Classroom

Maslow's Hierarchy of Needs categorizes human needs into five groups. The first is a physiological need or a need to feel good physically. Often this is associated with having adequate food and shelter. Next is safety, or a need a secure environment. There is also a social need, which includes elements of love and belonging, as a means of helping the individual complete their expected family roles and societal roles. After physiological, safety, and social needs have been met the next need in the hierarchical ladder is esteem. This may encompass social status, a need for respect from peers, and a well-identified self-image. Finally, there is the need for self-actualization, which is related to growth and development. Basic needs must be met first before you can begin to address high-order needs such as self-actualization.

Physiological Needs

Physiological needs are translated into a classroom or learning environment through the students' need to feel that they have all of the tools, techniques and resources necessary to be successful. For example, if you provide students with a textbook but do not provide them with additional resources to support the development of their skill sets, the very first or primary need will remain unmet and pose a challenge for the process of learning.

Getting Down To Business

Safety Needs

The next need is safety. An instructor can help students feel secure by creating a safe learning environment, where their opinions, beliefs, contributions, prior experiences and existing knowledge are valued and included during class discussions. While an instructor cannot establish or guarantee a physically safe environment, s/he can promote a perception and feeling of safety in the process of learning.

Social Needs

It may not seem that the student's social need can be met, because it is associated with love and belonging; however, an instructor can create conditions in the classroom that promote a sense of community. For example, group or team exercises can help students learn to collaborate, which will strengthen class discussions and create a sense of belonging.

Esteem Needs

Esteem is the status and respect with which human beings are regarded by their peers. Instructors who incorporate activities which assist students in achieving status and self-respect will support fulfillment of the esteem need. This can be accomplished by providing an environment in which students experience success because of their involvement in the class. Some learning theorists believe that success in itself is a solution to motivation and learning. Students experience success, and in turn feel that their need for esteem has been met. They understand that they have a capacity to learn and their instructor has helped them reach their potential. Helping students rise to the challenge may cause some of them to view you as a "tough" instructor.

There is a difference between being tough just for the sake of demanding compliance, and taking a firm stance to promote learning. You can be tough and fair at the same time, challenging students to do their very best. Students have a desire to learn and they have a perception of how the process takes place, often influenced by their prior academic experience. Some students believe that knowledge is given to them and others view it as something that they must acquire. Some believe that grades are given, while other students know that grades are earned. Because every instructor has a unique approach to facilitation, students begin to develop a generalization about what to expect when they start a new class. An instructor's interactions with them will either agree with or conflict with that expectation. Regardless of what students perceive about the process, it is important to help students do their best.

As students take classes and move through their degree programs, they develop a comfortable routine. When an instructor provides feedback, it is possible to discover that students have a capacity to learn more and perform at a higher cognitive level. As their awareness of this potential increases, they may need new skills or improvement in their existing skill sets. You need to show students that they are capable of developmental progress by helping them find relevant resources, tools and techniques. Students may feel that you are being tough, because you are pushing them out of their comfort zones.

Deciding students need an extra push is challenging for them and for you. Students may experience fear, frustration or feel singled out. As their instructor, you need to find ways to overcome their concerns and resistance. This means adapting feedback, evaluating the effectiveness of classroom interactions, and building strong working relationships. Being firm with students for the purpose of developmental growth, without attempting to demonstrate your superiority over them, is the mark of a good instructor.

If you decide to be demanding from a developmental perspective, remember the importance of also being fair and supportive. You can be a mentor and a guide to your students. You can provide a support system for your students through a caring attitude and a genuine interest in helping them improve their performance and develop their skill sets. You can also demonstrate your belief in them by being responsive to their needs for self-esteem. You are likely to transform their perceptions of self-esteem when they reach a point where they realize what they have learned and how they have progressed as students. Sometimes an extra push can lead the way for academic growth and enhanced motivation.

Self-Actualization

Self-actualization is the highest level on Maslow's hierarchy of needs. It is the adult's realization that they have experienced growth through their efforts and accomplishments. Students may not fully realize that this need has been met until the class has concluded and they have received their final feedback and grade. In fact, they may not realize it until sometime later, when they are in another class and discover they have acquired valuable skills and knowledge that has caused a personal and/or professional transformation.

The following suggestions can help you address your students' need for growth and success in the class:

- Offer problems, case studies or other challenges which require students to utilize critical thinking, reflection and analysis skills. Be sure that you offer your support, along with resources, tools and techniques to assist them.

- Treat your students as responsible adults. Help them to develop a strong sense of self-awareness, along with an ability to identify their needs and how they are being met through involvement in the class.

- Have an open mind to your students and their backgrounds. If you view all students as having a capacity to learn you will not be influenced by their present performance level and recognize where they are in need of skill set development.

- Be flexible with your students when extenuating circumstances arise. Find out what your institution's policies are and what flexibility you can offer your students when needed.

"Rubrics and Adult Learners: Andragogy and Assessment"

by Fred C. Bolton

Helpful Tips

Research Question and Method

Adult students might be expected to have a greater appreciation for rubrics because they reduce uncertainty; clearly articulate the issues that an instructor feels are important; and provide the student with a link between assignment, expected outcome, and learning objective. This hypothesis was tested with a sample of over 150 adult undergraduate and graduate students enrolled in accelerated business degree programs at Averett University.

Findings

Students repeatedly indicated that rubrics were useful in setting goals. A common comment was that rubrics "give you a guideline and show exactly what is expected." This helped students provide relevant content in assignments with little fluff or filler material.

Many students also commented that rubrics help "you know what the standards are when preparing assignments." By reviewing the criteria for evaluating performance, students could determine much of their grade before turning in an assignment. This reduced uncertainty and permitted an individual determination of the amount of effort needed for a specific assignment. From the instructor's perspective, rubrics provided considerable value. Through careful preparation of rubrics, critical issues that students should focus on were identified. This helped students pay more attention to primary content and reduced their efforts to add unnecessary material to assignments.

Assessment Update, Volume 18, Number 3, May–June 2006, pp. 5-6.

CHAPTER 3
STUDENT ENGAGEMENT —WHY IT MATTERS

Student Retention—Why It Matters

When you hear the phrase "student retention," what comes to mind? A set of numbers beyond your control? It is easy to view student retention, student satisfaction and student persistence as a responsibility of college or university administrators. The truth of the matter is that student retention is one of the most widely studied areas in higher education. In the 1970s, student retention was seen as a reflection on the individual student, her/his skills, and work ethic. College drop-outs were thought to be less able and less motivated. Students failed, not institutions.

Over the course of the past decades, that perception has changed dramatically. For example, our understanding of the experience of students of different educational, social and economic backgrounds has grown. Throughout these changes, one fact has remained clear: involvement, or what is commonly referred to as engagement, matters and it matters most during the critical first year of college. Part-time faculty are more likely to be employed to teach first year students, and so become important players in any institution's student engagement and retention efforts.

It is now a widely accepted fact that classroom faculty are key to institutional efforts to increase student retention. Student retention is everyone's business. However, research has made it clear that student retention is the business of the faculty in particular.

Students Make the First Choice

When a student decides to attend a particular school, it is often because of an interest in a specific degree program. As a means of attracting new students, schools promote programs, resources, services, features and other opportunities. Students often make an initial decision based upon their expectations of what they hope to accomplish and learn by earning their degrees. The reality of these expectations comes to light when students step into their classrooms and meet their instructors, meet you.

Instructors Reaffirm or Negate that Choice

The classroom environment an instructor creates helps students confirm, discard or adapt their expectations about the process of learning. When an instructor is responsive, students are likely to believe their developmental needs can be met. Instructors who create meaningful learning environments encourage student retention. However, the goal is not simply to keep students enrolled in their degree programs, but rather to focus on educational outcomes, where students create knowledge and develop skill sets through active participation in the process of learning. Student retention is sometimes an issue of persistence, because students may face significant challenges, such as academic preparedness, time management and self-motivation.

Retention is More than Numbers

From a developmental perspective one of the most important issues with respect to student retention is sustained growth—the student's ability to develop skill sets and acquire knowledge. From the student's perspective, there is an expected return on investment of time, effort and, of course, money. Student retention involves positive learning experiences and interactions with instructors. Recent research indicates that part-time faculty at community colleges can negatively impact the overall learning environment in a variety of ways:

• Part-time faculty offer less variety in their instructional practices, are unavailable for extended student learning and advising, and are less connected with colleagues and the institution (Community College Survey of Student Engagement, 2007).

Getting Down To Business

• Part-time faculty do not advise students as often, use active teaching techniques less often, spend less time preparing for class, and are less likely to participate in teaching workshops (Umbach, 2008).

• Part-time faculty under-prepare students and less often retain students in math and English for subsequent courses taught by full-time instructors.

• There is a negative impact on graduation rates at community colleges where higher percentages of part-time faculty are employed.

Recent research should, then, be interpreted by the part-time business instructor as an important cautionary message. There are hurdles involved with teaching part-time that are recognized and must be addressed in order to help students succeed.

 While an instructor may not be able to predict how students will react to their particular method of classroom facilitation; their attitude towards students and the conditions they create in the classroom will often determine if students continue their program. Student retention is not exclusively about numbers, it is the essence of interactions developed throughout the duration of the class. It all begins with the instructor.

Student Engagement 101

As an instructor do you expect that your students will be active and present in the class? The level of a student's involvement in the class and the learning process are often assessed by his or her performance and the work product submitted; however, does active involvement equal engagement in the class? What does student engagement mean to you and to your class? Instructors must understand the process of engagement.

Defining Student Engagement

Engagement is an action-based state that consists of the time, energy, and effort that the student devotes to his or her class. The process of being engaged in the class involves more than the student just getting by in his or her class or doing the minimum required to pass the course. When students are engaged, they are devoting the time necessary to become an active participant in the process of learning and their attention is focused on the course.

A student may consciously think about being engaged in the class or it may occur as a reaction to specific requirements, such as a participation requirement or a group project. It is possible for the level of a student's engagement to frequently change, depending upon the interactions and experiences with other students and the instructor. For example, if the student is feeling confident about her/his progress and abilities, that positive emotion can enhance engagement. In contrast, if the student feels discouraged engagement and progress may diminish.

 Adam Fletcher (2009) has found that "student engagement is increasingly seen as an indicator of successful classroom instruction."

Engagement may be enhanced or reduced if there is a feeling of being disconnected from the class or the instructor. Students who experience negative interactions may retreat from the class or withdraw their active engagement from the class as a reaction or retaliation for what they have experienced or how they have perceived a particular incident.

When adults experience engagement, they are devoting their full attention to the task and they are enthusiastically involved, highly interested and experiencing positive emotions. Active engagement can lead to increased participation in class discussions, which is a gauge instructors often use to measure the level of a student's participation.

Getting Down To Business

The Instructor's Role in Student Engagement

The process of learning itself may produce emotional reactions which can influence engagement. If an instructor encourages students to utilize critical thinking and reflection, students are likely to experience a range of emotions while exploring their opinions, ideas and belief systems. The process of critical self-examination can happen while the student is working on his or her own or during classroom discussions, emphasizing the need for instructors to provide support and guidance. Instructors must establish classroom conditions which encourage positive interactions in a productive, respectful environment. When students feel positive emotions and have positive experiences, they are likely to be fully engaged in the learning process and actively present in the class.

The instructor's level of engagement has a direct impact on a student's level of engagement. Students who believe their instructor is present and engaged will be more active and engaged in the class as well. When instructors demonstrate a high level of enthusiasm as they engage in the class, they provide an example for students to follow.

Dr. Richard D. Jones (2008) notes that "it is easy to observe the lack of student engagement when students are slouched in their chairs and not listening to the teacher or participating in the discussion." From the instructor's perspective, adult learner engagement may be observed but not measured as the instructor is often focused on the required assignments, class discussions and administrative aspects of classroom facilitation. In addition, many classroom assessments are designed to measure performance and progress towards meeting the required learning objectives rather than the level of engagement. Because student assessments are performance driven, engagement often becomes a criterion that is considered but not measured.

Increased engagement will have a positive impact on individual and classroom performance; therefore, instructors should consider methods of engaging students in the class.

Encouraging Student Engagement

Factors which frequently influence student engagement in any classroom environment include family, career responsibilities, students attitudes, prior class experiences, and perceptions about the class, their instructor and the ability of the course to meet their needs.

Dr. Richard Jones (2008) reminds instructors that "relevance can help create conditions and motivation necessary for students to make the personal investment required for rigorous work or optimal learning," and that "students invest more of themselves, work harder, and learn better when the topic is interesting and connected to something that they already know."

Class discussions provide an opportunity to add relevance as an instructor can connect students to the course topics by sharing real world examples, their own experiences, and supplemental resources which brings the course topics to life.

Tristan de Frondeville (2009) notes that "although it may take years to develop the repertoire of skills and lessons that enable you to permanently create this active-learning environment, you can begin by discerning which activities truly engage your students." If a learning activity does not generate students' interest then it is time to consider revising or eliminating that activity. While it is not possible to create excitement and enthusiasm for every class activity and assignment, it is important to consider if the activities are busy work or something relevant to the learning objectives and have a potential to enhance the process of learning.

Demonstrate Engagement for Your Students

Model active engagement in the class with daily participation postings, availability to address questions and concerns, and frequent communication. Students who have negative interactions with their instructor or other students may retreat from the class or withdraw their active engagement from the class. As noted within the article "Drivers of Persistence" by the New England Literacy

Getting Down To Business

Resource Center, "it is human nature that when we feel welcomed, respected, and develop a sense of belonging, we are more apt to return to the setting or endeavor than when those factors are not present. Instructors should convey passion and enthusiasm for the subject. When students see that passion, they want to participate. In a traditional classroom environment students physically observe their instructor's involvement in the class, along with their enthusiasm and passion. For the online classroom those characteristics are demonstrated through discussion boards and written communication.

Adam Fletcher (2009) has conducted a literature review of this topic and listed "five indicators for student engagement in college," which include "the level of academic challenge, active and collaborative learning, student-faculty interaction, enriching education experiences and a supportive learning environment." One method of addressing this list of indicators is to allow students to make choices concerning their assignments or involvement with the class as a means of encouraging them to feel that they had a choice in their level of engagement. For example, students could receive a list of possible topics for an assignment and choose one that is of interest to them. Another way to encourage engagement is to provide written feedback each week about the students' overall progress and discuss specific resources that address their developmental needs.

What does student engagement mean to you and to your class? Instructors have the ability to influence student engagement in the class by providing support and guidance, being actively present in the class, developing meaningful interactions and demonstrating engagement through their participation, passion and enthusiasm. The goal is to create a learning environment which encourages students to be involved, because students who are highly motivated to participate in the learning process are also engaged.

"Unmasking the Effects of Student Engagement on First-Year College Grades and Persistence"

by George D. Kuh, Ty M. Cruce, Rick Shoup and Jillian Kinzie

Conclusions, Discussion, and Implications

....Faculty and staff must use effective educational practices throughout the institution to help compensate for shortcomings in students' academic preparation and to create a culture that fosters student success (Allen, 1999; Fleming, 1984).

The classroom is the only regular venue that most commuting and part-time students have for interacting with other students and with faculty. Thus, using the classroom to create communities of learning must be a high priority in terms of creating a success-oriented campus culture.

Faculty members...must also be more intentional about teaching institutional values and traditions and informing students about campus events, procedures, and deadlines such as registration.

Faculty members also could design cooperative learning activities that bring students together to work collaboratively after class on meaningful tasks. Because peers are very influential to student learning and values development, institutions must harness and shape this influence to the extent possible so it is educationally purposeful and helps to reinforce academic expectations. A well-designed first-year seminar, freshman interest group, or learning community (where students take two or more courses together) can serve this purpose.

The Journal of Higher Education, Volume 79, Number 5, September/October 2008, pp. 540-563.

CHAPTER 4
EFFECTIVE STRATEGIES
FOR TEACHING ADULTS

Teacher Behaviors

Adjunct faculty can assist student learning with tried and proven strategies. Some principles and strategies to remember are:

- **The teacher is a facilitator of learning.** Students do not expect teachers to know all there is to know about the subject. They do expect, however, the teacher to facilitate learning the facts and skills of the course.
- **Understand your teaching situation.** As an adjunct faculty member you may have a variety of assignments at different institutions. When making your class preparations, consider the following questions: Is this class part of a competitive program? Are the goals clarified for the student and the institution? Can student projects be developed to meet the students' needs?
- **Allow for individual differences.** Every classroom will contain a diverse group of individuals. Allow for this by giving individual help, knowing students' names, and being aware of differing backgrounds.
- **Vary teaching activities.** Use different activities in the classroom. Try new ideas. Some experts recommend changing activities every 20 minutes.
- **Develop a supportive climate.** Students should understand that you are there to support them in the learning process not to prove how tough the course is.
- **Be sensitive to barriers.** Some of the baggage students bring with them include: unsuccessful previous educational experience, time restraints, confusion

concerning college (procedures) in general, failure to understand their academic limitations, stress, physical and mental handicaps.

- **Be a learning partner.** Communicate to the students that you are a partner in their learning. You will develop and work with them on strategy, materials and projects that will allow them to self direct their learning experience.
- **Emphasize experimentation.** Emphasize to the students that trying new learning techniques and making mistakes are often as valuable as reaching the right conclusion immediately.
- **Use technology to enhance learning.** Know about and be able to use the latest learning technologies.

Most of all it is important that you be understanding and considerate. With dynamic changes in the educational field today, you need to keep up with these technological and cultural changes so that they become part of the teaching/learning process. Being alert to these changes will prevent one of the worst student criticism, "it isn't done that way anymore."

Teacher Roles in a Collaborative Classroom

M.B. Tinzmann, B.F. Jones, T.F. Fennimore, J. Bakker, C. Fine, and J. Pierce (Oak Brook, 1990) provide us with an excellent overview of collaborative learning from the perspective of the instructor:

Across the nation, teachers are defining their roles in terms of mediating learning through dialogue and collaboration. What is important here is that these behaviors
(1) drive instruction in collaborative classrooms,
(2) have specific purposes in collaborative contexts.

Facilitating involves creating rich environments and activities for linking new information to prior knowledge, providing opportunities for collaborative work and problem solving and offering students a multiplicity of authentic learning tasks. This may first involve attention to the physical environment. For example, teachers move desks so that all students can see each other, thus establishing a setting that promotes true discussion.

A collaborative classroom often has a multiplicity of projects or activity centers using everyday objects for representing numerical information in meaningful ways and for conducting experiments that solve real problems. These classrooms also boast a rich variety of magazines, journals, newspapers, audiotapes and videos which allow students to experience and use diverse media for communicating ideas.

Facilitating in collaborative classrooms also involves people. Inside the classroom, students are organized into heterogeneous groups with roles such as Team Leader, Encourager, Reteller, Recorder and Spokesperson.

Facilitation vs. Teaching

There are various titles assigned to business instructors including teacher, professor, or facilitator. Online instructors are more often referred to as facilitators rather than teachers. When instructors are referred to as facilitators, this reflects the nature of adult learning and how the instructor is involved in the process. The principles of self-directed learning and andragogy foster the use of facilitation. Instructors facilitate the process of adult learning rather than providing direct instruction where they are simply telling students what it is they need to know. The word teaching, then, becomes synonymous with primary classroom instruction, this aligns with the principal of pedagogy or teaching children.

Regardless of the title you are given, as a business instructor you will discover there are elements of teaching and facilitation involved in the work that you will do in and out of the classroom. You are expected to encourage your adult students to participate in the class; you hold them accountable and responsible for their performance, and you teach them indirectly through your interactions and communication with them. Your specific title does not matter as much as the instructional strategies you implement.

When you are asked to consider your work as that of a classroom facilitator, the focus of your interactions with students will center on guiding them as they interact with and within the classroom environment. You are expected to provide tools and resources necessary for students to acquire knowledge, and develop clear academic skill sets. In essence, you are guiding students without directly teaching them. As a classroom facilitator, you are expected to be very involved and engaged in the class. You will develop meaningful interactions during class discussions, and provide consistent and frequent feedback which addresses students' developmental needs.

Your active participation in class discussions, along with your overall performance, set the standard. You become a model for students, and you must teach them to be self-motivated. When you hold students accountable for meeting assignment due dates, criteria and expectations, you teach them to take responsibility for their role in the learning process. While doing this, you must always follow and uphold your school's policies and procedures. When unsure about policies and procedure, refer to your faculty handbook (if one has been given to you or is available online) or ask your department chair. Never make up your own rules or apply existing rules capriciously.

You can teach your students how to learn and set them on a path of continued self-development and self-improvement. As an instructor, you will find that elements of teaching will always be part of the work that you do.

Student Behaviors

During your teaching tenure you will experience differing classroom behavior from students that may challenge your ability to maintain the class in a constructive and positive manner. Keep in mind that the following suggestions are simply observations of other teachers and may not apply to all situations.

Getting Down To Business

- **The class expert.** This person has all or most of the answers and is more than willing to share them—and will argue if he or she is not right. Make eye contact with a different student in the class and ask for an opinion. Allow other students to react. Give respondent time to tell anecdotes and/or present position, then remind the "expert" and the class that they must get back to the objectives of the course.

- **The quiet class.** Give positive reinforcement to any response from any student. Change teaching strategies and request an answer to a simple question at the beginning of the next class session. Use questioning techniques, group work, partner system, current events, personal experiences, brainstorming or icebreakers.

- **The talkative class.** Direct a question to a group or supportive individual. Quiet class in order to recognize an individual. Validate or invalidate her/his point and move to the next topic in the lesson plan. Allow time for conversation, specify time for class work to begin, exert your control.

- **The negative student.** Initially ignore! Invite the student to a conference, provide success experience, determine an interest of student and cultivate it.

- **The off-the-subject student.** Allow some freedom for discussion and for the reaction of other students. Other students will usually provide incentive to get back on subject. Seize the opportunity and stress the need to get back to course objectives.

- **The unruly student.** Remain calm and polite. Above all keep your cool and your temper. Don't disagree. Try to determine the student's position and his or her reason for concern. Listen intently and allow the student an opportunity to verbally withdraw from the situation.

If you encounter an angry student, determine the basis of the student's anger. Ask the individual to meet with you privately during the break and if necessary call an immediate break. As a last resort the class may be dismissed and institutional procedures for such a situation should be implemented. Keep in mind that your primary responsibility is the safety of all students. If procedures are not established, inquire of your institution why they are not.

Understanding the basics of adult learning principles helps an instructor become aware of how students interact with their classroom environment and more importantly, it explains the process of how adults learn as they participate in classroom activities and acquire knowledge. Because of the unique learning styles of adult students, there is a crucial need for focused classroom instruction and effective facilitation strategies.

Communication and Tone

One of the most important facilitation strategies you can develop as an instructor is the communication plan you use with your students. At times it can be challenging to find a method of relating to your students in a meaningful way. It can also be a challenge to develop communication techniques. A carefully planned communication strategy helps you communicate effectively with your students, engages them in the process, and encourages their willingness to participate constructively.

Classroom communication strategy begins with the first class session. Actively evaluate your students' experience, knowledge and background, and you will be better able to formulate effective strategies to communicate with them. On that first day, you are setting the stage for your students and letting them see how you will communicate with them throughout the semester. Student retention, performance and participation in a course are often an indication of how effective an instructor's communication strategy is.

Getting Down To Business

 Communication Rule: The message must be clearly received, processed and understood by the recipient. Well-developed messages connect you with your students. Pay careful attention to the words you use; avoid talking up or down to your students. Eliminate forms of exaggeration and generalization. Monitor the outcome or delivery of the message communicated.

The words you choose are as important as the content of the message itself. Your words convey meaning and emotion through the overall tone of the message. Your students will either connect with the message or lose interest. A sure way to connect with your students is to demonstrate professionalism and respect for them in all written communications. Avoid technical jargon and talking down to your students. Never allow negative perceptions, personal opinions, prejudices or biases to influence the wording of your message or its overall tone. Conversely, don't fall into the habit of trying to make your students feel good, or trying to win their respect through the use of flattery. By all means praise your students when they deserve it, but always keep it professional.

 Generalizations compensate for a lack of knowledge, facts or preparation. There's never anything wrong with telling students you will find the answer to a question that has you stumped.

The process of communicating effectively begins with your approach to developing messages, and concludes by monitoring how it has been received. Because communication occurs so quickly and may involve a large number of students, it may not be possible to evaluate every message composed and delivered. What you can do is watch for trends that are evident in students' responses to you and your facilitation of the class. When you take a proactive approach to communicating with students in the classroom, you develop powerful messages that connect you with your students and enhance your interactions.

Developing Strong Working Relationships

How you interact with students depends upon your approach to teaching and the goals you establish. Expect students to participate in the class, follow the directions you have established, and complete the required assignments simply because they are told to do so. However, their doing so does not guarantee a positive working relationship. Meaningful relationships are forged and nurtured. Your goal as an instructor is to create an environment that is conducive to learning and to identify ways to work with your students productively. Students will become motivated and interested in a class and class materials when they feel a connection to their instructor. When students are working with you, they are more invested in the class, more likely to focus, and they are often more willing to consider your suggestions and the developmental feedback you provide.

The following tips on how faculty can develop positive relationships with students come from the Teaching Effectiveness Program at the University of Oregon (http://tep.uoregon.edu/resources/faqs/issuesofrespect/positiverelate.html):

1. Respect and listen to your students.

2. Be dedicated and enthusiastic in your teaching.

3. Be able to do the work and understand the course material.

4. Do not be afraid to admit your mistakes.

5. Expect and praise good work.

6. When students have done well, tell them.

7. Be constructive in your criticisms.

8. If you do not know the answer, help them find it.

9. Be fair and consistent with all students.

At the very heart of adult learning is an interactive, developmental process which is enhanced when students work with you. Students need your feedback and personal guidance to continually make academic progress. Even though your students are self-directed by nature, your individualized attention to their developmental needs facilitates their growth. In the business classroom, in every classroom, students need conversations with you, interactions with their fellow students in the classroom shaped by you, as well as personalized feedback. These kinds of interactions encourage student peak performance and peak engagement in the class. The outcome is a natural increase in the motivation to learn.

Students who do not develop positive connections with faculty are often lost, literally and figuratively. Research published by the National Survey of Student Engagement reveals that students who are engaged with campus life earn higher grades, are more satisfied and are more likely to persist to graduation.

Another benefit of productive working relationships is that they will strengthen almost any message you deliver to your students, which includes your expectations for performance in the class. Strong relationships also facilitate the flow of communication in the class. This allows students to feel they can ask questions and express their concerns. When students trust that their instructor is approachable and willing to listen, they become more open to constructive feedback.

As you consider the relationships that you have with your students here are several questions you can ask which will assist you as you develop a strategy to build meaningful and productive relationships:

Figure 4.1 Working Relationship Checklist

1. Do you respond to students' questions and concerns in a timely manner?

2. Do you offer feedback by summarizing strengths and areas of needed development, while offering resources to address student needs?

3. Do you acknowledge your students' contributions to class discussions?

4. How do you challenge your students to increase their capacity to learn?

5. Do you encourage your students to participate in the process of learning?

6. Do you utilize questioning techniques which help students develop a greater understanding of the course topics?

7. Do you establish classroom conditions which allow students to participate in the process of learning?

8. Do you encourage students to ask questions about the class and their progress along the way?

Time Management Strategies

As an instructor you must manage your time effectively and always be well prepared for class. This is particularly true if you are an adjunct facilitating business classes part-time while balancing other responsibilities and career-related duties. On campus each week your duties are likely to include overseeing the basic operations of your class, participating with students in class discussions, developing feedback that is focused on your students' developmental needs, monitoring class conditions, and maintaining a supportive learning environment. Completing these duties requires a significant investment of your time, which means that you must find tools and techniques that will allow you to meet these requirements productively, efficiently and effectively.

Required Duties:——————————————————————————

——

Due Date:——————

Date Completed:——————

Feedback:——————————————————————————

——

——

Participation:——————————————————————————

——

——

——

Figure 4.2 Time Management Review

It's time to develop a time management plan or review the effectiveness of your existing time management plan. The table on the preceding page provides you with a format to review your current facilitation duties and evaluate how you budget your time to meet these responsibilities. Start by picking one week from your current class, or a class that you recently completed, and fill in the chart.

Did you discover anything new about the amount of time it takes to complete your required facilitation duties? Did you experience stress at any point during the week while you were trying to complete these requirements? Were there any required facilitation duties that you did not complete or that you had to complete in a hurry because you were short of time? Did you have any pending projects that you are unable to complete? Overall, what aspects of managing your time worked well? Were there any aspects that did not work well and how could those issues be addressed in a productive manner?

 As you develop a time management plan, build your weekly time allotment based upon a set of clearly defined teaching goals. For example, do you want to budget enough time to complete just the essential facilitation requirements or is your goal to complete your duties *and* monitor the development of a meaningful learning environment?

A weekly time budget will keep you on track and help you avoid procrastination. As you budget or allocate time for your facilitation duties, you can also break down more time-consuming duties into smaller chunks that can be easily managed throughout the work week. You will discover pockets of unexpected or available time throughout the week and those periods of time can be utilized to work ahead, and evaluate the progress you've made with the items that have the highest priority for the week. The students will have seen how well-prepared and efficient you were and understand your teaching style. A good teacher is recognized as one who is well prepared, has a good knowledge of the subject, and shows a passion for teaching.

CHAPTER 5
COMMUNICATING WITH STUDENTS

Keep Information Flowing

Communicating with students is one of the most important and potentially complicated tasks facing any college business instructor. There are a variety of tools available beginning with a simple course website. Many colleges use course website systems, including Moodle, an easy-to-use system with an emphasis on communication, collaboration and student involvement. Colleges also create their own course web site "hubs." Check with your department chair about the course website creation tools available. There are also a number of other internet-based modes of communication including email, Facebook, blogs and Twitter.

Blogs

The days of the one-size-fits-all classroom are history. Using blogging in the classroom is a less conventional way to capture the attention and interest of kinesthetic learners. They're given something to do with their hands, they are stimulated, and they learn in a forum outside of the traditional classroom setting. Blogs might be the first assignment some of the students have ever turned in on time, and you may be surprised by the results.

Brownstein and Klein point out that blogs may be used as virtual environments, where all students may participate in critical discourse on specific topics. In many ways blogs are similar to web forum postings. Since blogs are well-accepted methods for communicating one's thoughts or ideas, or responding to other people's postings, they are now being used by many college and university professors, although because of their fairly recent appearance on the scene there is little research published on their uses and their effect on student learning.

Communicating With Students

Brownstein and Klein (2006) write that, "Blogging gives voice to students who often feel uncomfortable speaking up in class and can have a powerful impact on a greater number of students in the classroom as it supports more learning styles." They have identified a noticeable change in the quality and quantity of learning taking place in the classroom since introducing blogs. In particular, the focus has moved from "what" to "why."

Blogs offer another format for communications in a classroom, and, given their current popularity, will continue to be electronic communication tools of use in teaching.

Twitter

This tool, like blogs, has potential in teaching and learning, although the limited length of responses (140 characters) does not allow for detailed discussions. However, a recent study at the University of Leicester in the UK discovered that Tweeting helped: "Develop peer support among students, develop personal learning networks, and helped students to arrange social meetings."

The researchers also found that Twitter was very attractive as a data collection tool for assessing and recording the student experience, with a wide range of free and increasingly sophisticated on-line analysis tools (Cann et al., 2009).

 In the 2012 report, "Twitteracy: Tweeting as a New Literary Practice," Christine Greenhow, a Michigan State University professor and coauthor of the study, found that students who were actively engaging with classmates and the instructor on Twitter were more interested in the course material and ultimately received higher grades.

Getting Down To Business

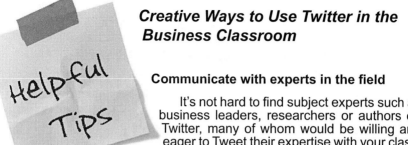

Creative Ways to Use Twitter in the Business Classroom

Communicate with experts in the field

It's not hard to find subject experts such as business leaders, researchers or authors on Twitter, many of whom would be willing and eager to Tweet their expertise with your class. A simple search on Twitter can connect you with experts on any topic in business you're teaching.

Monitor the learning process

Students' grades improve when everyone is engaged in monitoring the learning process. Get your students involved by asking them to Tweet and reply about questions they have, observations they've made, and ideas they have about their course materials.

Create scavenger hunts

Students can search the Internet for websites, images and documents that match your rubric or unit objective, and then post these links to Twitter. Once a resource is up, then another group is not allowed to post it, thus motivating the students to work in friendly competition with each other toward a common goal.

Present bite-sized pieces of information

Another great use for Twitter is to teach isolated chunks of information that can be learned in any order and in small amounts. You can set up your own Twitter account dedicated to just one topic, solely for dispensing information, without links or class interaction. Some examples of bite-sized information are: study tips, historical facts, business theory, vocabulary words – anything you can think of!

Engage students in current events

Have your students use Twitter to report real-time news events to the class. An example might be to set up an account just for Tweeting current events. One idea might be for students to Tweet a required amount during a certain time period (two per week, for example), with no two students ever Tweeting the same news story.

Recreate history

A creative way for students to study history is to research and write imaginary tweets for a historical character. Once they do this, they can use other websites such as HootSuite to schedule the tweets and Wallwisher to post and receive feedback. It's an engaging method of research and the students will have an audience for the work; this is also an excellent way to collaborate with other classrooms and schools.

U.S. News University Directory (http://www.usnewsuniversitydirectory.com/)

Communicating With Students

Social Networking Sites

Sites such as Quora, Pinterest, Academic.edu, Google+, Tumblr, Snapchat, Instagram, LinkedIn, YouTube, Facebook and MySpace are popular social networking sites. While these sites have a potential for use in education settings, it is not clear that they have immediate applications to teaching. However a number of instructors do use video clips which are posted on YouTube in their lectures, and it's possible to maintain pages on Facebook and Twitter for use by students in their classes to communicate with other classmates and the instructor.

Learning Management Systems

There are a number of different companies marketing learning management software, including Desire2Learn and Blackboard. Usually, a college or university has a license for all of the campus so the instructor may not have a choice as to which system to use. These systems have a number of different components including:

- Posting class notes/videos

- Links to external websites

- Class web forum

- E-mail to instructor

- Posting class notices

- Example tests

- Class marks register

- Links to other educational software packages such as Second Life, blogs etc.

Second Life

"Second Life is a free on-line multi-user virtual environment (MUVE) that allows users to meet in virtual space, build and manipulate virtual objects, and converse via text or voice over internet protocol (VoIP)" (Atkinson, Wilson and Kidd, 2008).

Second Life allows for the creation of virtual classes where each user assumes a virtual identity, an avatar, which can be controlled by the user. Students create their own avatars and remain anonymous. This allows students who are quiet in a live, on-campus class, to use their avatars to ask questions, make statements and join in discussions which they might not do in on-campus classes. Second Life may be used as an adjunct to a lecture class or a distance education course. The software may also be used to create three-dimensional simulations, models, demonstrations which students can manipulate, interact with, or store for later use. "Different campuses host different types of events, such as scheduled lectures, media screenings, theatrical productions, labs and virtual office hours. Practically anything possible in real life is possible in SL" (Atkinson, Wilson and Kidd, 2008).

Second Life offers an interesting alternative to live classes whereby students, and instructors, can assume virtual, anonymous, personalities. Hundreds of North American colleges and universities use Second Life.

Student Response Systems

One problem associated with large classes particularly is gauging student understanding of the material presented. While some students will ask questions about material they do not understand, it is usually only when marking tests and examinations that the instructor can see whether students really have understood the material presented in class. The recent advent of electronic clickers presents an opportunity for instructors to check during class whether or not students understand the material being presented. Clickers present us with a new, instantaneous feedback system. Herreid (2006) writes that, "They provide instant feedback to students and faculty regardless of the size of the class, and have a clear value in socialization, making impersonal classes more intimate. The technology also seems to resonate with students fascination with interactive media."

Clickers are like television remote controls, with numbered buttons that students can push to give an answer, usually to a multiple choice question. Each student's response is transmitted to a receiver which picks them up and feeds the response into a computer. The class results can be viewed by the instructor on the computer screen. The instructor can quickly gauge the level of understanding of the students and can re-teach the material if the clicker responses indicate a less than ideal understanding of the material. Herreid points out that, "Research on various forms of instructional feedback, all of which can be provided by clicker systems, has indicated direct relationships between feedback and improved student learning (Guthrie and Carlin, 2004)."

Duncan (2005) lists eleven ways in which instructors can use clickers:

- to measure what students know prior to instruction;

- to measure student attitudes;

- to find out if students have done the reading;

- to get students to confront misconceptions;

- to transform demonstrations;

- to increase students' retention of the material they have been taught;

- to test students' understanding;

- to make some kinds of assessment easier;

- to facilitate testing of conceptual material;

- to facilitate discussion and peer instruction; and

- to increase class attendance.

Textbooks often come bundled with electronic clickers so textbook choice may determine which type is used.

Even though there are only a few published assessments of clicker use, because of their novelty, Herreid (2006) writes that,

- student enthusiasm for clickers is high;

- student attendance is strikingly improved, changing from

below 50 percent in the lecture method to over 80 percent when clickers are used;

- student learning appears to be improved;

- faculty enthusiasm is high; and

- student apathy is much less evident.

While there are some disadvantages of clickers (cost, steep learning curve for faculty etc.) Herreid (2006) concludes that these are minor when compared to their advantages.

If you don't have access to electronic clickers don't despair. You can get most of the advantages of them using non-electronic response systems. I have seen paper/cardboard cubes with different letters and/or colors on each side used to the same effect. When the instructor poses a question, students show (to the instructor) the side of the cube which displays their chosen response. If colored cube sides are used the instructor can quickly estimate how many members of the class have answered the question correctly, and then decide whether to move on to new material or to go over the previous material again.

First Time Teacher Revelation #27

CHAPTER 6
CLASSROOM TEACHING TECHNIQUES

Once you have made the decision concerning your objectives for the course, the next step is to choose the instructional methods and strategies necessary to carry them out. In examining these teaching strategies and techniques, you should ask yourself the following questions:

- When should I teach by demonstration and when should I encourage students to try it themselves?

- When should I explain important topics and issues verbally and when should I prepare handouts for discussion?

- When should I lecture and when should I use question-and-answer strategies?

- When should I use audiovisual aids to support my points in discussion and lecture?

- When should I utilize multimedia technology and associated strategies to enhance my teaching?

Successful teaching depends to a certain degree upon the initiative, creativity and risk-taking prowess of the instructor. Even instructors with these characteristics, however, must use a variety of techniques and approaches to be successful.

Classroom Teaching Techniques

Some of the more common techniques used by successful teachers include:

Instructor-Based Techniques	**Student-Based Techniques**
Lectures	Active learning
Discussions	Cooperative learning
Question/answer sessions	Inductive learning
Demonstrations	Buzz groups
Guest lecturers	Problem-based learning

Out-of-Class Activities
Outside reading assignments
Projects
Case studies
Field trips
Journal/publication readings
Term papers/research projects
Internet research

The Lecture

According to Bligh (2000), so ingrained is the lecture in higher education, that over 95 percent of humanities and science professors in the U.S. use it as their main teaching method in spite of all the research showing that students do not learn well in lecture situations.

A study at the University of California at Berkeley (Angelo, 1991) has shown that college students only remember 20 percent of what they hear from a traditional lecture or demonstration several days after the class. Furthermore, this study also found that, in a room full of dozens of students, fewer than 15 percent are paying attention to what is being presented at any one time during the class, not counting the first eight minutes of a class when a much higher percentage of students are following the lecture.

The major reason for this is that students do not expend much energy thinking about what is being discussed in a traditional-style presentation. Students may also be so busy writing notes (or playing on their laptops) that they don't have the time to think about what they are actually doing.

Getting Down To Business

It reminds me of a cartoon I have, showing a student returning home from school and telling his father, "They don't give us time to learn anything; we have to listen to the teacher all day." How very true. This does not mean that we should suddenly abandon lectures make the best use of the time we have in a class to ensure students are actually learning. Otherwise, we might find that the following saying is all too true: "With the lecture, the information usually passes from the notes of the instructor to the notes of the students without passing through the minds of either!"

One thing that greatly influenced my own teaching when I became aware of it was the issue of student attention span in the *What's the Use of Lectures* book by Bligh (1971). The following graph shows the typical decrement curve for a person's attention to a single task over a period of time such as a lecture period.

This pattern is usually displayed in the level of performance of students during a lecture. It has been suggested (McLeish 1968; Lloyd 1968) that student attention rises and falls in the last five minutes of a 55 minute lecture. Not surprisingly the student level of attention is highest at the start of a lecture but begins to decline thereafter, and around 10-20 minutes into the lecture the level of attention begins to decrease dramatically and continues

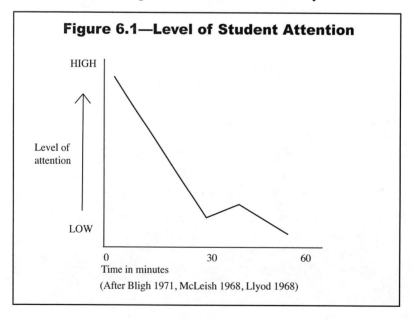

Figure 6.1—Level of Student Attention

HIGH

Level of attention

LOW

0   30   60

Time in minutes

(After Bligh 1971, McLeish 1968, Llyod 1968)

to decline for the rest of the hour until the last five minutes. In fact student attention has been shown to drop off after only 10 to 15 minutes (Hartley and Davies, 1978). This suggests that the attention span of an average student might only be around 10-15 minutes during which time the most learning takes place.

Bligh (1971) notes that several studies have found a marked improvement in attention after a short break. Figure 6.2 shows the effect of a rest or change of activity on the level of attention after a break of a few minutes. If there is such a rest period for a few minutes, when the lecture resumes, the amount of effective learning is almost as high as it was at the start of the lecture. Again, the amount of effective learning will drop off during the next part of the lecture.

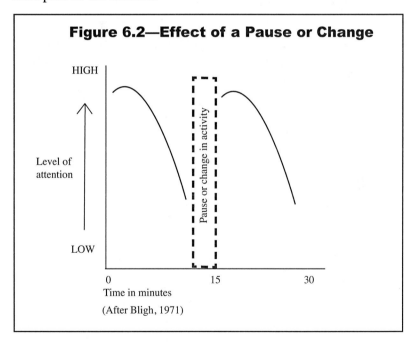

Figure 6.2—Effect of a Pause or Change

A number of studies have examined the efficacy of pauses during a one-hour lecture period, and these all confirm that students are more attentive during the lecture period, and do better on subsequent tests.

Ruhl et al. (2007) point out that the pause may also benefit the lecturer since he/she may use the pauses to scan the lecture notes and, perhaps, improve the quality of his/her delivery after the pause.

Try it out for yourself! Inform your class that you will teach for 15 minutes and then take a two-minute break. During this break students should review their notes to see if there was anything they didn't understand, and discuss it with a neighbor to see if the neighbor could explain it to them. If not, the student can ask questions on the material after the break. The two-minute break allows students to socialize with, and get to know their neighbors, and will give you a few minutes to get organized for the next part of the lecture.

Several years ago, to try out the strategy I used the two-minute pause with a single class during an entire semester, and when the grades for all the sections were tallied at the end of term, that section performed significantly better than all the others. And why wouldn't they? I had taught in smaller chunks of time, when student learning was most effective. Since that initial trial run, I've continued to use this technique when lecturing.

 When talking to colleagues about my use of this technique, they often comment that I have *lost* four minutes of instructional time in a fifty-minute lecture! Of course, what is most important is not the *quantity* of teaching time, but the *quality* of the student learning.

It is important to point out that Bligh's graph (Figure 6.2) points to a change of activity after approximately 12-14 minutes. Good teachers employ more active techniques to allow students to become better involved in their own learning. Such activities might include solving problems you present to the class, small group discussions, demonstrations, and a variety of other techniques dealt with in this book.

It is perhaps also worth noting that Bligh (1971) reports that the rate of decrement (i.e., loss of attention) is steeper for more difficult subject matter and, therefore, the more difficult the lecture material the more frequent the pauses or variations in teaching should be. Bligh also points out that the same decrements in attention occur during the course of a day.

 While some people reach their optimum level of performance during the morning, and others at midday, very few people are at their best in the afternoon. Thus, attention to lectures is more difficult in the afternoon and evening. Lectures delivered at those times should be shorter, more varied, and more stimulating, should give way to small group teaching and other active methods of learning.

There are general guidelines to keep in mind when presenting the lecture. Although they are basic and well known, they are worth repeating here.

- Make certain your lecture is organized and presented in an orderly manner. Too often students are critical of instructors who appear to be rambling.

- Using illustrations throughout the lecture is an indication of a well organized lecture which the presenter is taking seriously.

- It is important that you remember to speak clearly and directly to the audience.

- Give mental breaks every ten minutes or so.

- Change the procedure by using an anecdote or activity so that the lecture is not a continuous one-way dialog.

- If you have a tendency to use distracters or mannerisms such as "you know" or "OK", be aware and avoid them.

- Use the chalk board, overhead, smart board or any prop that you feel appropriate to enhance your lecture.

- Finally, do not hesitate to build "thinking pauses" into your lectures so your students have time mentally to catch their breath.

Getting Down To Business

Discussion

Class discussions lead to higher-order learning. They also allow students to identify problems and to use other members of the group as resources. This is especially important in today's diverse classroom, where older, experienced adults and younger students may be sitting side-by-side in your class.

Reflect on your participation in class discussion and your students' involvement. Ask yourself the following questions:

- Do students actively participate in my classroom discussions?

- Are my students engaged in the process of learning because of their interactions with me and other students?

Class discussions have the potential to enhance the learning process when the course materials and topics are brought to life through the knowledge and experiences shared by you and other students. Creating an environment which successfully transforms discussions into meaningful interactions requires advanced planning and focused participation on your part.

Discussion Facilitation Strategies

One of the most powerful methods of transforming class discussions into meaningful interactions is through the use of follow up questions designed to encourage exploration of the course topics. These questions can be built around the students' contributions, with the inclusion of theory and real-world examples, while encouraging students to utilize critical thinking skills. Questioning students is an important tool for stimulating classroom participation and motivating students. Experienced instructors make it a rule to question as many different students as possible during a class session.

Besides encouraging student participation and arousing student curiosity, questioning students is an effective way to gauge their preparation for class as well as their progress and understanding of the class topic. Eliciting answers can develop students' confidence in their self-expression. The right choice of questions can also encourage higher order learning such as analysis, synthesis and evaluation. There is hardly a disadvantage associated with questioning if good judgment is exercised. Appropriate timing is important; pace the questions so students have time to phrase their answers. For example, it would be ineffective to continue to question a student who is embarrassed or is having difficulty responding. Such students need to be "brought along" in the classroom. Good questioning involves several strategies:

- Use open-ended questions when possible, that is, do not use questions which have a yes/no answer.

- Use questions which elicit a comment or additional queries from students, even to the point of saying to a student, "What do you think of that?"

- Questions should be part of the lesson plan. Prepare them ahead of time and don't wait for them to "happen."

- Different types of questions have different purposes. They are usually found in four categories: knowledge, content, discussion and stimulation.

- A knowledge question: "What is a spreadsheet?"

- A content question: "What are the functions of a spreadsheet?"

- A discussion question: "What are the advantages and disadvantages of using a spreadsheet?"

- A stimulation question: "How can spreadsheets enhance your job accuracy?" This may be followed with "Why do you think this?"

Whenever possible, questions should be addressed to individuals by name rather than to the whole class. If your class is giving you the silent treatment, a quick question and answer can bail you out. This strategy also encourages students to ask questions of their own. Skillful questioning stimulates students to respond with contributions which demonstrate more sophisticated reasoning.

Getting Down To Business

Remember to move through course material at a pace that allows adequate time for student questions. Sometimes instructors move so quickly through the course material that they don't appear to have time to consider a student question.

 Some instructors may actually say "hold your questions until the end of class." This is not only discouraging; it also runs the risk that the student will forget a question valuable to the class discussion.

To encouraging questions from students:

- Show complete respect for any questions or comments made by students;

- Specifically ask students questions during the presentation;

- Use probing questions with the students;

- Ask students if they need clarification on issues;

- Ask students to give the pros and cons of a particular issue or point;

- Have other students ask questions concerning the response.

Discussions in the Business Classroom

Class discussions have the potential to become meaningful interactions when students are interested and, more importantly, they are contributing ideas and information. An instructor can help the process by encouraging students, particularly adult students, to consider how the course topics relate to their professional experience, interests, professional needs and academic goals. Listen to students' responses for an understanding of their thought processes, and how they are interacting with the course materials.

Discussions must be planned just as carefully as any other learning activity. There are faculty who "wait for discussions to happen." This may result in no discussion or off topic discussions. One helpful discussion technique is to start with a common experience. The experience might be a current event, a common problem to be solved or a controversial issue. It may be necessary to place students in small groups, give them a topic and have them find a solution or develop a hypothesis.

Make sure that you give all students the opportunity to speak. If there is a lull in the discussion, let the silence continue. There are students in the class who will feel a need to break the silence. Urge students to talk to each other and not just to you. Be aware of students who do not participate, draw them in by asking them to respond to their classmates' comments.

In the interactive classroom, remember that you are a facilitator of learning—more so than almost than any other situation.

Group Projects—A Must in the Business Classroom

Further engage your business students with group work. Group work not only breaks up an extended lecture, it creates an interactive element to the class, transforming students from passive recipients to active participants. Instead of hearing about the course topics, students are provided with an opportunity to directly interact with those topics in a meaningful way.

When students work together, you will find that they will begin talking to each other and developing a sense of collaboration and community. Instructors may be concerned that some students may not be willing to participate in a group activity or assignment. Students are often more willing to talk in small groups. This will also help your students develop a team building skill set that will be beneficial for their career as well. Most organizations require employees to be able to interact with and communicate effectively with others.

Getting Down To Business

Group projects are a learning tool and a means of bringing the course concepts to life. During a class lecture, you can explain the basics of a particular business theory or course topic, add videos or other supplemental resources to enhance your lecture and then add your own expertise, background, knowledge and experience. By working as a group, students have an opportunity to further interact with the information provided.

Group work enhances collaborative learning through participation and sharing. Group interactions increase student confidence and help them develop a sense of connection to other students. Never assume that because students may work in various organizational settings they have fully developed their communication, presentation, or team-building skills.

 Make certain that all group work is keyed to specific course materials and concepts, and not just "busy work."

Classroom Conflict: Prevention and Resolution

Class discussions can be a source of conflict as students express diverse views, personal beliefs and opinions. Instructors must create respectful learning environments by establishing ground rules for the class discussions.

To maintain an effective learning environment, an instructor must take the lead during conflict resolution discussions and model dynamic communication. Acknowledge what has occurred then discuss the reasons why miscommunication, perceptions or hurt feelings may have resulted. Your sincerity and choice of words will have a powerful impact.

Make a clear distinction between dispute and conflict. Focus on issues rather than emotions, while encouraging an open and respectful dialogue. A dispute occurs when there is a disagreement about an opinion, belief, fact or position on a topic. A dispute is short-term in nature. An unresolved dispute can become a conflict. Conflicts disrupt learning.

Classroom Teaching Techniques

 Stay alert. The first sign that there is the potential for a dispute among students is when there is a breakdown in communication. This can happen during classroom discussions, as well as during group work.

Address disagreements quickly. Help students move past their initial reactions and find common ground that allows them to work together effectively. When working with students to resolve disputes, help them separate facts from opinions and feelings.

CHAPTER 7
PREPARING FOR THE FIRST CLASS

As you prepare for the start of a new class, review your contractual requirements, facilitation expectations and instructional duties so that you are prepared and have a time-line developed. Individual responsibilities will vary between schools, but there are basics that you are likely to have for the start of each new class. The checklist below should be reviewed prior to the start of each new course.

Figure 7.1 Class Preparation Checklist

- Do I have names and information for important contacts?

- Are there any meetings I need to attend?

- Am I familiar with the required school policies?

- Do I have learning objectives for the course?

- Do I have the required textbook and course materials?

- Do I have supplemental resources to enhance learning?

- What is the grading policy and when are grades due?

- Is there an evaluation form for the course?

- Am I aware of faculty contractual obligations?

- Do I have a copy of the academic calendar?

- Have I developed learning activities, including discussion starters?

- Do I have a feedback plan in place, including the development of rubrics?

- Are class lectures prepared?

- If teaching online, do I have all of the first week postings prepared?

- Is the course syllabus ready for the first day of class?

Planning Your Business Course — In a Hurry!

As the checklist suggests, ideally, planning for teaching a course should start well before the first class of the semester. However, for many of you this will not be possible since you will receive your teaching assignments a day or two before the start of the semester, or maybe after the start of the semester when the designated instructor fails to arrive for their assignment! So what can you do when you are given a last minute teaching assignment? Hopefully the department has a course syllabus for you from previous semesters, the textbook has already been selected and is available to students in the institution's bookstore; if not, you really are behind the eight ball. Under such circumstances how on earth are you going to give a good first class when everything seems stacked against you? After all first impressions are the ones that count.

First of all you will need to have a course syllabus, or an outline, ready to give to your students in that first class. At a minimum it should include the course number and title, the name of the textbook (and hopefully the chapters to be covered), the assessment methods for the course (tests, examinations, assignments etc.) and finally information about yourself (name, office number, telephone number(s), email address, office hours etc.) If you don't have enough time to produce printed copies for each student, write the information on the board, or on a PowerPoint slide. Post the information to your course website if you have created one.

Once this routine administrative-type information has been covered, introduce yourself to the class, where you are from, where and what you studied at college/university, and maybe even your research topics for master's and/or doctoral degrees.

Getting Down To Business

If you feel comfortable enough doing so, talk about your work experience, your reasons for teaching and anything else that you think might be of interest to the students and which gives them some insight about you as a teacher and a person.

Depending on the size of the class you may wish to employ an icebreaker activity for students to get to know each other. As an example, students could get into pairs (or threes or fours) and each could introduce themselves, their background, interests, intended degree program and the reason why they are taking this particular course. At the end of the exercise, each student is then asked to "introduce" their partner to the rest of the class. Obviously this only works with small classes. In larger classes you might just wish to ask students to introduce themselves to their neighbors on both sides.

Another possible short exercise is to ask each student, anonymously or otherwise, to write down something about themselves, such as the degree they are hoping to complete, their previous background in the subject (none, high school etc.), the reason they are taking the course, the other subject(s) they are taking that semester, and any other interests they would like to add (sports, hobbies, other interests, possible careers etc.). These should be anonymous for you to read later on to get an idea of the class, which can help in the way you teach that particular class.

 Always do some teaching in the first class meeting so that students learn something about the subject, the way you teach and conduct classes. There are instructors who use the first class to introduce the course and themselves to the class and then finish. They don't do any teaching until the second class. Start the way you intend to continue, that is to teach.

Preparing for the First Class

I am reminded of a neighbor who was enrolled at university for the first time. When classes actually started he was looking forward to learning a new subject, but the instructor spent the whole of the first class talking about the administrative aspects of the course and never talked about the subject or gave a lecture. My neighbor came out of that class really disappointed that he had not learned anything about the subject he was so looking forward to studying. It is worthwhile remembering that while there will be students whose only interest is getting out of the classroom as quickly as possible there are those there who actually come excited to learn.

Another option, if you haven't had a chance to prepare even a short lecture, is to ask the students about their prior knowledge of the material you will be covering in the second class. This would serve as an opportunity for students to recall information from a previous course and, if nothing else, helps students to get back into a study mode after their vacations and to recall information they should have learned in previous classes or in the workplace. If students are not prepared to answer your questions publicly, you could even try this exercise as an individual or, even better, as a group test. At the end of the test you can ask how many scored at least 50 percent, 75 percent and even 100 percent. At least this way you will know how much background or pre-requisite information you will need to provide in the second class.

The Course Syllabus

When Erikson and Strommer (1991) asked students at the end of their freshman year what instructors might have done to help them, one of the three most frequent responses was to "provide a better syllabus." These authors say that a good syllabus will let students know "where the course will take them, how they are going to get there, and who is responsible for what along the way." Lewis (1994) says that a good syllabus will probably be more than two pages long and will contain the following:

Names, number and required texts, (i.e. course title and number, classroom and time slot, instructor's name, office, phone number, office hours, text titles and how they are to be used, etc.)

Getting Down To Business

It will also include:

- Introduction to the subject matter and course goals

- Description of evaluation procedures

- Overview of class activities and assignments

- Course outline (including week-by-week schedule of topics, readings, assignments; exact dates of exams, assignment deadlines etc.)

- Course policies (including policies for attendance, make-up work, late assignments; statements about student conduct in large classes.)

Lewis's suggestions for the syllabus are excellent and should serve as a good guide for a syllabus. Since these suggestions were published before the general acceptance and use of email and other computer-based technologies I would also add to her list the email address of the instructor, class web site, blog address, and other social network technologies used with the course. I would also add a plagiarism policy to the list of course policies.

Figure 7.2—Sample Course Syllabus

Achievement University
Syllabus
Name of Course: Principles of Marketing
Instructor: Dr. Dennis
Office: B151
Phone: 987-5037 (Office)
dennis@ccc.edu
Class website: http://www.ccc.edu/marketing/Denis
Dr. Dennis on Twitter: @DrDMarketing
Office Hours: M-F 9:00 to 10:00
M,W, F: 12:00 to 2:00 (by appointment)
Lecture hours: 3

TEXT BOOK & SIMULATION HANDBOOK
1) W. D. Perreault, Jr., J.P Cannon, and E. J. McCarthy, 2009, *Basic Marketing: A Marketing Strategy and Planning Approach*, (17th ed.), Irwin/McGraw Hill. 2) C. H. Mason and W. D. Perreault, Jr., 2002 *The Marketing Game!* 3rd edition, New York: McGraw-Hill.
Class requirements:
All papers must be submitted electronically. Papers may be revised for a higher grade. Use the MLA format for all papers. Plan to spend three to four hours each week writing.

Course description: Marketing is a dynamic and an exciting field, a key tool in confronting the challenges American enterprises are facing at home and abroad. In this course you will learn about the "real" nature and scope of marketing management of which advertising and sales are simply two facets. You will be introduced to other aspects of marketing, such as:1) Marketing Strategy, 2) Promotion, 3) Market Planning, 4) Distribution, 5) Industrial Marketing, 6) Retailing and Wholesaling, 7) Target Marketing, 8) International Marketing, 9) Market Segmentation, 10) Services Marketing and 11) Pricing.

Exams and Quizzes: Three exams (two midterms and one final exam) and two quizzes have been scheduled for this section of marketing management. Make-ups for the examinations will be given only for the most extraordinary and documented reasons. The exams will consist of both multiple-choice and essay questions.

Term Paper: This is a writing intensive course. Term paper will be used to improve your writing skills. In this individual term paper, you will be developing a marketing plan for your simulation company. In order for me to provide feedback to you on your written paper, you are asked to turn in two preliminary reports during the semester. These reports also have to be typed and there is no minimum page limitation.

Grading System: Course grades will be based on exams, quizzes, the marketing simulation, written report and contribution and participation. Details are illustrated below:

2 Exams	120 points
2 Quizzes	60 points
Final Exam	100 points
Marketing Simulation (Group)	40 points
2 Written Paper Drafts	10 points
Written Term Paper (Individual)	50 points
Participation	20 points
TOTAL	400 points

Course Rules and Procedure:

Class Attendance: Students are expected to attend classes regularly, be punctual, and complete all work whether present or not. Whenever possible, the opportunity for making up class-work missed as a result of an excused absence is to be worked out between the instructor and the student upon the student's initiative.

Make-Up Exams: No make-up exams will be given for other than instructor approved absences. There are no excused absences from exams other than physician-documented illness and documented personal emergency.

Academic Honesty: All university, college and department policies on academic honesty will be strictly enforced. The usual consequence of academic dishonesty is failure of the course and referral of the case to the Dean for additional disciplinary action.

Figure 7.3—Sample Course Outline

Achievement University
Basic Statistics 101 Course Outline

I. Introduction
    A. Basic statistics—use and purposes
    B. Data gathering
        1. Instruments
        2. Recorded data
        3. Machine utilization

II. Presenting Data
    A. Tables
        1. Summary tables
            a. Table elements
            b. Tables with averages
    B. Graphs
        1. Types of graphs
            a. Bar
            b. Pie chart
            c. Line graph
        2. Data presentation with graphs
    C. Frequency distributions
        1. Discrete and continuous
        2. Class intervals

III. Descriptions and Comparison of Distributions
    A. Percentiles
        1. Computation of percentile
        2. Inter-percentile range
        3. Percentile score
    B. Mean and standard deviations
        1. Computation of mean
            a. From grouped data
            b. From arbitrary origin
        2. Variance formulas
    C. Frequency distributions
        1. Measures of central tendency
        2. Symmetry and skews
        3. Bimodal distributions

IV. Predictive or Estimate Techniques
    A. Regression
        1. Graphic application
        2. Assumption of linearity
    B. Correlation
        1. Computation of correlation coefficient
        2. Reliability of measurement

C. Circumstances affecting regression and analysis
    1. Errors of measurement
    2. Effect of range
    3. Interpretation of size
V. The Normal Curve and Statistical Inference
    A. The normal distribution
        1. Mean
        2. Standard deviation
        3. Characteristics
    B. Statistical inference
        1. Employing samples
            a. Randomness
            b. Parameters
        2. Normal distribution
            a. Standard errors
            b. Unbiased estimate
            c. Confidence interval
    C. Testing hypothesis
        1. Definition of statistical hypothesis
        2. Test of hypothesis
            a. Level of significance
            b. One-sided test
        3. Computing power of test

The Lesson Plan

A lesson plan is a must for all teachers because it acts as a reference and guide for each class meeting. A flexible lesson plan allows for discussion of appropriate current events and provides a backup system if multimedia materials or equipment do not arrive or suffer a mechanical or electrical malfunction. The plan contains important questions and quotes from supplemental material not contained in the text, and should include definitions, comments on the purposes of the class, and student and teacher activities.

Lesson plans reflect your creative endeavors and unique abilities as a teacher. Often, the syllabus and, to some extent, course outlines are dictated to faculty. The demands for accountability and institutional goals sometimes restrict these two documents. Lesson plans, however, allow greater flexibility and permit techniques and strategies unique to the instructor, including appropriate personal experiences and anecdotes.

Preparing for the First Class

After determining your objectives, outline the major topics, including definitions and references to sources not in the textbook, in your daily lesson plans. Your lesson plan may include everything you need to take to the classroom such as notes, handouts, thumb drives, computer disks, software references, etc. (Stephan, 2000). Shown in figures 7.4 and 7.5 are examples of a lesson plan format and a sample lesson plan. Effective course planning includes constructing a plan for each class meeting. Number the lessons, place them in a loose-leaf binder, and maintain them as a record and a guide for activities.

Figure 7.4—Suggested Lesson Plan Format

Course number and Name_____Date_____
(after first page simply number chronologically)
Session #_____
Definitions to be covered_____
_____
Class objective(s)_____
_____
Student activities or exercises_____
_____
Instructor activities_____
_____
Major impact or thought_____
Assignment_____
_____

Figure 7.5—Sample Lesson Plan

Course number and name: Algebra 101   Date_____
Session #9
Definitions:
1. Equation is a statement that two expressions are equal
2. Expression is a mathematical statement
3. Linear equation is equation of 1st order
Class objectives:
1. To demonstrate equations through the use of various expressions of equality
2. To prove equality of expressions through technique of substitution

Student activities:
1. Complete sample problems in class
2. Demonstrate competence of sample by board work

Instructor Activities:
1. Demonstrate validity of solution of equations
2. Assure student understanding through personal observations of seat and board work

Major impact: Understand the solution of basic linear equations.

Assignment: Problems—Exercise 8, pp. 41-42.

Course Objectives

Even though it takes time to write up good objectives, they are useful in a variety of ways. Not only do the students know exactly what is expected of them, but it is then easier to construct tests and exams, since the questions are phrased to see if students have achieved these objectives. Behavioral objectives are also useful in deciding how and what to teach as the course material should cover them. Sometimes you may find that the objectives, as written, are impossible to teach, and students to learn, and/or to test, in which case it may be necessary to revise the objectives. You can also start each class by telling students which objectives you are dealing with that day.

Use Supplemental Materials

Course materials provide instructors with an effective starting point for facilitation of the class. Through the process of interacting with these resources it may become necessary to find supplemental materials which help connect students with the course topics. Instructors will find it helpful to periodically review the sources used from the students' perspective and consider adding timely and relevant resources to enhance class discussions and deepen the interactive process of learning.

As the class progresses, instructors should use supplemental materials such as articles, website links or additional books. Supplemental materials further students' understanding of core concepts. In a traditional classroom, instructors have an opportunity to deliver a lecture, which allows them to present information directly to the students in an environment where they can offer insight, guidance and clarification. In an online classroom, students are expected to find the materials and then demonstrate that they are able to interact effectively with that information.

For the online classroom, instructors may consider enhancing the course materials provided by developing their own overviews and summaries. The lecture-based approach to classroom facilitation can be adapted to the online classroom through the use of an overview or preview message. These messages help students look ahead to the upcoming week, the key concepts to be explored and can offer tips, pointers and suggestions to help prepare students for interacting with the materials. After the class week has concluded, provide a summary or wrap-up that helps students reflect on the learning objectives that should have been met. Use a wrap-up message to summarize key points addressed in the discussion boards and important topics that students should be familiar with from the assigned readings and materials.

When an instructor considers adding resources, it is important to evaluate the relevancy, source and credibility of the information. Ideally, articles should be peer-reviewed. Websites must be evaluated by examining such criteria as the author's credentials, affiliations and potential for bias. Acquiring supplemental materials is also a learning activity. Have your students find scholarly sources. Current and relevant materials add depth to the class, the discussions and the overall process of learning.

Policies

You may also find it useful to prepare in advance some time-saving procedures, particularly for remarking tests. Develop a hand-out which explains your procedure for remarking tests. A copy of my sheet appears below. You can adapt it to your own needs.

Getting Down To Business

Grade Reviews

Figure 7.6—Sample Grade Review Policy

Principles of Marketing 240

GRADE REVIEW POLICY

If you are of the opinion that your paper has been incorrectly marked, you may appeal the marking by following the these procedures.

1. If the problem is a mathematical error in adding up marks, indicate this problem at the top of the front page and hand in your paper to have the mark adjusted.

2. If the problem is a disagreement with the mark(s) assigned to one or more answers, document on a separate sheet of paper why you think that your answer(s) is worth more marks by reference to the marking scheme. You should refer to class notes, rubric, textbook etc. as and when appropriate.

While every effort is taken to ensure that all assignments are graded in the same way, there will inevitably be some discrepancies. Papers that are to be re-graded should be handed in no later than two weeks after the papers are returned. *Papers will not be re-graded after that date.*

 Students miss tests for a variety of reasons (medical, attending other "official" events, taking part in sporting events etc.). Develop a policy statement explaining your procedures for dealing with these absences.

Plagiarism

It is essential to have a policy related to plagiarism. While many institutions have official statements on what plagiarism includes, and how instances of plagiarism are dealt with, it is useful to explain these policies to students. If the institution does not have a policy, prepare a statement for your class. There are a number of different software companies marketing plagiarism-detecting programs (i.e. Turnitin.com). Some colleges and universities use such software programs to check student assignments.

Surviving The First Class

No matter how long you have been teaching you will always be faced with another "first class." If it is your very first time teaching the strategies you incorporate are not significantly different from those used on the first class of any future course you may teach. There will always be some level of anxiety before the first class begins. For experienced instructors who have just completed a course where rapport and communication had been developed, you now face a new class, the unknown. Remember: you never get the second chance to make a first impression, and this is nowhere more true than in the world of teaching.

Arrive early and come fully prepared. If possible, visit the actual classroom before and figure out how to correctly use the audiovisual equipment. Pay attention to the small details. For instance, make sure you know how to turn on/off the room lights and have a working microphone if the room requires the use of an amplifier. If you intend to distribute materials to the class, have them available at the door and hand them out as students enter.

Stand by the door of the classroom on the first day. Personally welcome each student as they arrive and hand out any printed materials that are to be distributed. Obviously, this type of welcome is easier to do with a small class, but it's worth the effort as it gives the impression that you're interested in having the students there.

At the start of a new class, I briefly introduce myself and the course, and make reference to the evaluation scheme. I then tell the students that I will be teaching this period. I give an overview of what I intend to cover (behavioral objectives, concept map etc.) and then start to teach. I teach for approximately 12-14 minutes and then take a two-minute break (having explained its real purpose). After that, I give another mini-lecture.

I finish the class with a student activity as a way of allowing them to get to know their classmates and to indicate that my classes involve students in their own learning.

The students will have seen how well-prepared and efficient you are, understand your teaching style, and that you involved them in a student-centered activity. A good teacher is recognized as one who is well prepared, has a good knowledge of the subject, and shows a passion for teaching and their subject and so it is important to convey these characteristics in the first class. Show your enthusiasm for teaching, your subject and your interest in students.

"Jitters. Butterflies. Nerves."

Helpful Tips

by Melissa Miller, Ed.D., M.Ed., AdjunctNation.com, originally published September 28, 2010

I landed my dream job of teaching part-time. This is what I had worked so hard for – years in the classroom and going back to school for my Ed.D. While I was excited, my nervousness surprised me! I was prepared, I had the academic and professional experience, and I had experience as a student. Why was I nervous?

Maybe I was nervous because I badly wanted to do a good job? I had been out of the workforce for a year, and I was feeling slightly "rusty." Would I be able to keep up and still be a relevant, engaging and fun teacher? Maybe I was nervous because I was not sure how much time was going to be required in order for me to do a good job? I had a general idea of how much time the job was going to involve, but this was one of many unknowns that I faced.

I had the training, the technology skills and the pedagogical skills, of course, but I was unsure about the reality of really teaching and educating in a college classroom.

The night before my first class, I gave myself a pep talk. I focused on how I was prepared and reminded myself that my experience and knowledge had led me to this point. I focused on how I wanted to share my experiences and knowledge with adult learners and this helped ease my nerves.

After my first class, I was so excited! It felt good to be back in the classroom with motivated learners. I had so much fun! When I went back and listened to my lecture (a practice I recommend for all new teachers whenever possible), I can sense my nervousness, but I don't think the students noticed. Well, at least they were polite enough not to say anything….

CHAPTER 8
TEACHING LARGE CLASSES

"We've raised the student cap."

It is almost inevitable that teaching undergraduate business courses, particularly introductory courses, means teaching large classes. There is a significant difference between the way in which a class of 300 is taught as compared to a class of 30 or 50 students.

Teaching a large class is not just a matter of teaching more students at the same time, for the larger class is taught in a larger room with fixed seating, and the extra students make even simple things, such as handing back test papers and assignments, more time-consuming. In addition in large classes students feel anonymous, and are less likely to contribute to classroom discussions.

In their study of large classes Wulff et al. (1987) noted that students commented on the impersonal nature of such classes which led to decreased motivation. Students also reported an increase in noise and distractions ("Rude people who come late, leave early, or sit and talk to their buddies."). Cooper and Robinson (2000) write, "It is a sad commentary on our universities that the least engaging class sizes and the least involving pedagogy is foisted upon the students at the most pivotal time of their undergraduate careers: when they are beginning college."

Large class size brings at least three sets of problems: a more challenging teaching environment, more time-consuming administrative tasks and a large anonymous, less involved audience. This chapter will give you some ideas as to how to tackle these challenges and some practical examples of how to teach large undergraduate classes.

The Lecture Hall

A large lecture hall is different from the average classroom. This is why you should visit the designated lecture room ahead of the first class to get acquainted with the space. In most such venues, one's voice needs assistance to be projected to the back of the room, so most lecture theatres are fitted with microphones, amplifiers and speakers. If you are using a portable microphone, remember to check the "low battery" warning light, it's important that your microphone not die on you mid-lecture.

Lewis (1994) suggests that you write something on the chalkboard, and then go to the back of the class to see if you can read it from there. Get used to writing large, three inches (eight centimeters) is about the *smallest* you can get away with in a lecture theatre situation. Similarly, if you use an overhead projector (still a useful piece of equipment even though it is an "older" technology), or even PowerPoint slides, try to use a font and size which can be read easily, even in the back row.

Next, find the light switches and dimmers. Check to find out where other relevant controls are positioned (speaker volume control, electronically operated screen, etc).

 Is your lecture hall equipped as an electronic teaching room containing a computer, a projector CD/DVD player, Wi-Fi access and a visual presenter? If so, arrange for training in the use of all of the equipment provided.

You should also make certain that the appropriate software is on the computer to run your program. More than once I have checked that everything else worked before a lecture or presentation only to find that the correct software was not on the computer.

One of the most useful pieces of equipment in large lecture rooms is the visual presenter. This piece of equipment does away with the need to produce overhead transparencies. With one of these electronic cameras you can project directly from the typed page without the additional step of producing costly overheads. Since the camera can also zoom in and out, one can even project directly from the printed page in a textbook or journal and use the zoom to magnify the image. I have even projected 35 mm color slides (rapidly becoming another obsolete technology) using the camera. Most instructors use PowerPoint (or an equivalent software package) to project their notes, pictures and graphics.

Administration

Large classes can also be very time-consuming due simply to the number of people in the class. For example, in a small class of, say 40 students, you could hand back marked tests and assignments by calling out the names of each of the students. Try handing back 200 papers that way! So how best to deal with collecting and distributing tests and assignments?

Ask students to place completed papers in piles marked in alphabetical order. Return the marked papers in a similar fashion, asking the students to come and pick up their papers at the end of the class.

 Don't hand back tests or papers during your teaching time in class. Students will be distracted by the materials.

Lewis (1994) suggests that the following areas are ones in which an instructor may wish to consider streamlining:

1. Developing and duplicating handouts, exams and homework problems;

2. Handling out and collecting those handouts, exams, and homework problems;

3. Grading homework and exams;

4. Keeping track of several hundred student grades;

5. Providing timely feedback to students;

6. Getting questions from students and providing them with answers;

7. Managing office hours.

Keeping Students Engaged

Teaching a large class in a lecture theatre can bring problems of interactivity with students. Yazedjian and Kolkhorst point (2007) point out that, "Students who believe they are anonymous often feel less personally responsible for learning, are less motivated to learn and are less likely to attend class." Lewis (1994) writes that, "Because large classes provide a great deal of anonymity, students frequently feel that they can talk to their neighbors, come or leave when they feel like it, and so forth, without suffering any kind of consequences."

Getting Down To Business

Lewis suggests that instructors make a statement about their expectations of the students and their responsibilities to themselves and to their fellow classmates. Sometimes, students feel that the back of a large lecture theatre is a place to sit and chat with friends, or even a convenient place to have lunch when they are not even taking the course. Some lecture halls I have visited were so noisy that it was almost impossible to hear the instructor.

Much of the problem of uninvolved students is the teaching method employed. While this book does describe a number of different instructional strategies, many of them are not easy to employ in a large class situation. Almost inevitably, the lecture is the instructional method most usually employed with large classes.

 But if one is lecturing a large class, how does one make students interested and hold their interest? Enthusiasm for your teaching and for your subject is the **key**.

As Weaver and Cottrell (1987) note, "If there is one instructor characteristic related to learning it is enthusiasm....The simplest person, fired with enthusiasm, is more persuasive than the most eloquent person without it."

If you are going to hold students' attention, it is important to vary the presentation. Interspersing a lecture with audiovisual materials, demonstrations and short student activities all help to keep students' attention.

A two-minute pause every 12-15 minutes or so, is a good way of restoring student energy, allowing the students a break from writing and gives them an opportunity of reviewing their notes and discussing them with their classmates (See Figures 6.1 and 6.2). Interspersing the lecture with a variety of student-based activities is important in any teaching situation, but is especially important in large classes.

You should have a number of activities ready to use at different times of the semester, but if you are new to teaching develop a few to try out and each semester add new ones so that you eventually have quite a few to use as circumstances permit.

The easiest ones to try are these three:

- Short demonstrations (especially if you have a student or two to assist you)

- Setting problems for students to solve individually or in groups

- Small group discussions to answer questions you pose

Remember that if you don't have an activity to use in a particular lecture period, you can always employ the two-minute pause, making the purpose of the pause clear to the students.

In a large class, remember that the class is probably very heterogeneous and has a wide variety of learning styles. Try to address all the learning styles during the course of a lecture. Thus, in addition to talking, which addresses the aural learning style, make use of visuals such as overheads, PowerPoint slides, models etc. to address the needs of visual learners. Kinesthetic learners are more difficult to accommodate in a large class situation, since they need to handle items and move around. Strategies that involve them in demonstrations are important.

Facilitating Discussions in Large Classes

Since students in large business classes are less likely to want to make comments or ask questions in front of their peers, you may have to elicit communication.

One way is to ask students to form small groups to discuss a question posed to the class and then to ask groups to give an answer. While it is not feasible to ask every group for an answer, you will receive a fair number of answers. Students in the small group format may be more willing to speak in the larger classes. This question/answer strategy can be used throughout the semester. As it becomes a familiar activity, more groups will be prepared to offer answers. You can get almost instantaneous feedback from students with electronic "clickers," or non-technological versions such as cardboard cubes with different responses on each side, or even colored cards (with different colors on the two sides).

Another interesting idea from Lewis (1994) is the use of question boxes placed near the door(s) in which students can place their written questions or comments, and which the instructor can answer in the next class. Of course, as was discussed in Chapter 5, there are a variety of technology-based options for students to ask questions, make comments and the like including e-mail, web forums, blogs, Twitter etc....

Other simple feedback options include the one-minute paper and the class questionnaire. Lewis (1994) suggests the one-minute paper given at the end of class asks the students to answer two short questions:

1. "What was the most important idea you learned during today's class?"

2. "What questions do you still have about the material discussed today?"

Another option, the brief questionnaire, takes students about five minutes to complete. Student response groups, a small group of students with whom the instructor meets every two weeks, is another tool that may be used. Other class members are encouraged to pass on their comments to the response group. You can even have informal open coffee sessions. Invite students to have coffee and discuss the course with you.

Tests and Assignments

Clearly, testing and marking written assignments for large classes can be a challenge. Here are a number of tips that can help make the task a bit less daunting:

1. Use a number of tests/exams but don't count all of them in calculating a student's final mark. Under this scheme, students can drop a low score, or can miss a test without you having to give *any* make-up exams.

2. Have a protocol/policy in place to deal with students asking for re-reads of papers, and stick to it. (See Figure 7.6 "Sample Grade Review Policy")

3. Written assignments do not have to be onerously long. Assign 1000-word writing projects and/or micro-themes.

4. Use an assignment rubric. Not only does it make marking much easier, but it also reduces significantly the numbers of students asking for their assignments to be regraded since they can see where their strong and weak points are.

5. If you have the use of TA's (teaching assistants) do not use them for grading subjective responses on tests and assignments – it will result in too much variability in grading standards. Use them to mark the more content-style questions. You should be the one to grade written assignments and essay questions.

Heppner, in *Teaching the Large College Class* (2007), writes, "Teaching large classes well is the most difficult and challenging task in academia and offers the fewest tangible rewards. Knowing, however, that you have a real, positive and inspiring effect on hundreds or thousands of young people will more than compensate for the liabilities. Do it right and you will have former students all over the world who will be grateful to you for the wisdom you gave them."

Getting Down To Business

Teaching Large Classes and Lectures

Helpful Tips

1. Ensure that course materials and resources are accessible to all by following the Universal Design for Learning model.

2. Be active in the classroom/auditorium. Move around the class and invite participation. This will help create an encouraging environment so that neither you nor your students will feel intimidated by the numbers.

3. Personalize your class; get to know as many names as possible. Extend your availability, show up to class early and be sure to keep regular office hours.

4. Integrate active learning strategies that are focused on specific outcomes. Consider using "clickers" for attendance, quizzes and to generate discussions.

5. Encourage participation by building things into the lesson that are generally not an experience one could get in other ways; debates, guest speakers, films, etc.

6. Create working teams or small groups of students for discussion and in-class work.

7. Put a "help" box in the classroom so that more reticent students can ask course or homework questions anonymously; budget time for your response at the beginning or end of the next class meeting.

8. Provide feedback to students often; short quizzes, outlines, bibliographies, summaries, etc.

9. Utilize teaching assistants effectively, both for administrative duties, such as attendance, and instructional duties, such as facilitating group work.

10. Creative student projects, whether for extra credit or as part of the requirements, can help personalize the course experience, making students feel more invested.

From: The Center for Teaching and Faculty Development, San Francisco State University (http://ctfd.sfsu.edu/)

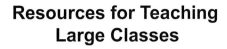

Resources for Teaching Large Classes

Bain, K. (2004). *What the Best College Teachers Do.* Cambridge, Mass: Harvard University Press.*

Carbone, E, and J. Greenberg. "Teaching Large Classes: Unpacking the Problem and Responding Creatively." In: *To Improve the Academy*, Vol. 17, 311-316. Stillwater, OK: New Forums Press.

Cooper, J.L. and Robinson, P. (2000). "The argument for making large classes seem small." In MacGregor, J., Cooper, J.L., Smith, K., and Robinson, P. (Eds.), "Strategies for energizing large classes: From small groups to Learning Communities." *New Directions for Teaching and Learning*, 81, 5-16.

Davis, B.G. (2009). *Tools for teaching* (2nd Ed.) San Francisco: Jossey-Bass.*

Gibbs, G. (1992). *Teaching more students: Problems and course design strategies.* Oxford: Oxonian Rewley Press.

Heppner, F. (2007). *Teaching the large college class: A guidebook for instructors with multitudes.* San Francisco: Jossey-Bass.

Stanley, C.A., and Porter, M.E. (2002). *Engaging large classes.* San Francisco: Anker.

Faculty Focus (website). Strategies for Teaching Large Classes - https://learn.unt.edu/bbcswebdav/pid-254763-dt-content-rid-1160615_1/xid-1160615_1.

Nicol, D., & Draper, S. (2008) Redesigning written feedback to students when class sizes are large (pdf). Paper presented at the Improving University Teachers Conference, 29 July - 1 August, Glasgow.

Schreyer Institute for Teaching Excellence. Teaching Large Classes (website). http://www.schreyerinstitute.psu.edu/Tools/Large/. Provides resources for breaking up your lecture, assessing students' understanding and engaging them in learning.

CHAPTER 9
BUSINESS STUDENTS & WRITING

Business writing has to be direct and to the point. So even business students with good writing skills in high school and college will have to learn a new style appropriate to the business world. From one student who boasted of having "severed" customers on a résumé, to the many more who insist on referring to managers as "mangers," the English language can be a struggle for some business students. So, amid complaints from employers, colleges and business schools are putting more emphasis on writing. This means business instructors need to be prepared to focus on writing skills.

Developing Written Assignments with a Purpose

Written assignments engage students in the process of learning, whether they are asked to write something in class or as homework. Written assignments help students demonstrate progress, knowledge acquisition, cognitive abilities and academic skill sets. This provides an instructor with an opportunity to assess students' developmental needs, provide resources and adapt teaching methods as needed.

From the student's perspective, written assignments provide the opportunity for self-directed learning, allowing students to take responsibility for their involvement in the process of learning. When students recognize the purpose of an assignment, its relationship to the course, the learning outcomes, and more importantly their academic and/or professional needs, they will likely respond positively.

Written assignments can be categorized in terms of the length of the assignment. Shorter written assignments will allow you to assess your students' progress for the week. Short writing assignments may take the form of an in-class written assessments or short homework projects. These assignments may be completed individually or in assigned groups. Shorter assignments are typically summary-based, overviews, such as short emails or memos.

Longer, narrative written assignments may also be completed individually or as a group. (In these assignments, students demonstrate subject matter expertise, analysis and provide informed and substantive responses.) This form of written assignment involves higher forms of cognitive processing and the use of critical thinking skills. Students are expected to demonstrate strong business writing skills in their responses.

Providing feedback for these assignments requires an investment of time for instructors. One must carefully evaluate the content of the response, the mechanics of the students' writing and monitor papers for originality.

A Step by Step Approach to Building Assignments

The most effective assignments are those which have been developed through a process of careful planning, anchored with a definitive purpose. The following steps present a process to help you create meaningful assignments.

Step One: Learning Objectives

The starting point for the development of written assignments originates from the learning objectives. Here are questions you can ask yourself to begin the process:

- What objectives have been established within the course syllabus?

- What are the specific learning objectives for this week?

By starting with the course objectives and weekly learning objectives, you create a quality assignment. The objectives establish parameters through which you can assess your students' progress. When you determine specific desired outcomes, you establish an effective comparison point and the assignment becomes a measurement tool. You should also keep in mind any expectations your institution has regarding students' written assignments. Does your institution hold expectations regarding skill sets that students should demonstrate when submitting a written assignment? If so, this needs to be a consideration when developing your assignments.

Step Two: Identifying A Purpose

After establishing the overall guiding objectives, the next step in a well-developed plan involves establishment of an identifiable purpose. Begin by asking: "What is the purpose of this assignment?" You can clarify this question with these follow-up questions:

- What do I want students to demonstrate?

- What knowledge do I expect them to have acquired?

- Which skill sets do I expect them to demonstrate?

A clearly defined purpose helps determine the content and length of a writing assignment. Another important consideration is the level of cognition you want students to utilize. Do you want them to utilize knowledge recall or higher forms of cognitive processing such as synthesis and analysis? (Bloom's Taxonomy defines six levels of cognition as described in Chapter 2.) Students begin with the basic level of cognition, knowledge, which includes remembering and reciting information. This is also called lower-level thinking.

The goal for a series of written assignments is to move students through the cognitive levels, into higher-order thinking, including synthesis and evaluation. For example, ask students to research a topic and ,through additional assignments, apply the information to a real-world problem and develop solutions.

Once you have determined the cognitive skills to be emphasized, develop a working structure, including a description of the primary learning activity involved. In addition to individual one-time written assignments, develop projects in a series, building one upon another.

Step Three: Determine Possible Outcomes

Work through the steps involved to understand the students' perspectives and the possible outcomes. This will allow you to anticipate any potential issues and provide clarification as needed. As you consider possible student responses, ask yourself the following questions:

- Does the expected outcome effectively demonstrate that the learning objective has been met?

- Do the possible outcomes align with the overall guiding purpose?

Step Four: Developing Instructions

The next step is to develop the assignment instructions. By planning the assignment ahead of time, you'll be able to provide clarification students may need during your class. Use prompts within the instructions such as "how," "what," "give an example," "explain," "define," "analyze." The instructions must clearly state the steps to follow and the prompts need to match the level of cognitive process you expect from your students. As you create the assignment instructions, develop a list of resources.

Step Five: Develop A Rubric

Develop a rubric for all written assignments. This provides students with a road map and you with an objective check-list. You will use the rubric to allocate points earned and explain how the grade was assigned. Generally, instructors allocate 60 to 75 percent of the total grade for the actual content of the response. The remaining portion of the grade is based on the writer's mechanics, including formatting, sentence structure, grammar, punctuation and spelling.

Getting Down To Business

Utilizing Rubrics

Students expect that their instructor will do more than provide a cursory overview or response to written assignments. Evaluating students' writing requires the instructor to consider multiple aspects, from the content of what was written to the mechanics and overall presentation of the response. It is helpful to have a structure developed for addressing this challenge. Rubrics offer uniform and meaningful feedback for all students.

The initial development of a rubric takes time. This is an opportunity to clearly define the assignment criteria and overall expectations. The assignment instructions often indicate what a student is to do for their assignment. A rubric expands on assignment instructions and offers an explanation regarding how the written assignment should be structured. The rubric outlines elements such as: topic development, word count, associated learning objectives, formatting guidelines, requirements regarding mechanics that include spelling, grammar and sentence structuring.

The rubric can also include specifics to guide students through the process of cognitive development with action words including: analyze, synthesize, evaluate, describe, develop, consider, contrast and identify.

 With a rubric students will have a clear understanding of how a writing assignment is evaluated and points earned. Rubrics transform an instructor's subjective feedback into objective and constructive feedback focused on established criteria.

The wording within a rubric serves as a foundation for an instructor to build upon through detailed comments in each section.

Figure 9.1—College Level Writing Rubric

College-Level Writing Rubric

	Masterful	Skilled	Able	Developing	Novice	(Way Off)
Focus, Purpose, Thesis (Controlling Idea)	Engaging and full development of a clear thesis as appropriate to assignment purpose.	Competent and well-developed thesis; thesis represents sound and adequate understanding of the assigned topic.	Mostly intelligible ideas; thesis is weak, unclear, too broad, or only indirectly supported.	Mostly unfocused ideas; little or no sense of purpose or signs of confusion; misunderstanding of the prompt; thesis is essentially missing or not discernable.	Ideas are extremely simplistic, showing	Shows complete confusion about the topic or inability to grasp it; thus conspicuous absence of thesis and lack of purpose.
Ideas, Support & Development (Evidence)	Consistent evidence with originality and depth of ideas; ideas work together as a unified whole; main points are sufficiently supported (with evidence); support is valid and specific.	Ideas supported sufficiently; support is sound, valid, and logical.	Main points and ideas are only indirectly supported; support isn't sufficient or specific, but is loosely relevant to main points.	Insufficient, non-specific, and/or irrelevant support.	Lack of support for main points; frequent and illogical generalizations without support.	Clear absence of support for main points.
Structure, Organization	Organization is sequential and appropriate to assignment; paragraphs are well developed and appropriately divided; ideas linked with smooth and effective transitions.	Competent organization, without sophistication. Competent paragraph structure; lacking in effective transitions.	Limited attempts to organize around a thesis; paragraphs are mostly stand-alones with weak or non-evident transitions.	Organization, while attempted, was unsuccessful. Paragraphs were simple, disconnected and formulaic. No evident transitions or planned sequence.	Organization, if evident at all, is confusing and disjointed; paragraph structure is weak and transitions are missing, inappropriate and/or illogical.	Paragraph structure does not exist; or is a single rambling paragraph or series of isolated paragraphs.
Audience, Tone, and Point-of-View	Clear discernment of distinctive audience; tone and point-of-view appropriate to the assignment.	Effective and accurate awareness of general audience; tone and point-of-view satisfactory.	Little or inconsistent sense of audience related to purpose; tone and point-of-view not refined or consistent.	Shows almost no awareness of a particular audience; reveals no grasp of appropriate tone and/or point-of-view for given assignment.	Lacks awareness of a particular appropriate audience for assignment; tone and point-of-view somewhat inappropriate or very inconsistent.	No evident awareness of audience as appropriate to assignment; tone completely inappropriate to assignment.
Sentence Structure (Grammar)	Each sentence structured effectively, powerfully; rich, well-chosen variety of sentence styles and length.	Effective and varied sentences; errors (if any) due to lack of careful proofreading; syntax errors (if any) reflect uses as colloquialisms.	Formulaic or tedious sentence patterns; shows some errors in sentence construction; some non-standard syntax usage.	Sentences show errors of structure; little or no variety; no grasp of sentence flow.	Simple sentences used excessively; almost exclusively; frequent errors of sentence structure.	Contains multiple and serious errors of sentence structure: i.e., fragments, run-ons. Unable to write simple sentences.
Mechanics and Presentation	Virtually free of punctuation, spelling, capitalization errors; appropriate format and presentation for assignment.	Contains only occasional punctuation, spelling, and/or capitalization errors. Few formatting errors. Most errors likely careless.	Contains several (mostly common) punctuation, spelling, and/or capitalization errors. Several errors in formatting or formatting is inconsistent.	Contains many errors of punctuation, spelling, and/or capitalization. Errors interfere with meaning in places. Formatting incorrect in most places.	Contains many and serious errors of punctuation, spelling, and/or capitalization; errors severely interfere with meaning. Formatting weak.	Frequent errors in spelling and capitalization; intrusive and/or inaccurate punctuation, communication is hindered. No formatting as appropriate to assignment.
Vocabulary and Word Usage	Exceptional vocabulary range, accuracy, and correct and effective word usage.	Good vocabulary range and accuracy of usage.	Ordinary vocabulary range, mostly accurate; some vernacular terms.	Errors of diction, and usage, while evident, do not interfere with readability.	Extremely limited vocabulary; choices lack grasp of diction; usage is inaccurate.	Diction and syntax make communication meaningless or very confusing at best.
	Masterful	**Skilled**	**Able**	**Developing**	**Novice**	**(Way Off)**

Getting Down To Business

 Never provide a rubric without comments. Through written notations, it is possible to engage the student in a conversation that acknowledges effort and progress, while encouraging the student to consider overall strengths and areas of needed improvement.

Share a copy of the rubric prior to the assignment due date to further emphasize your expectations and give students a way to self-evaluate their written work. A well-evaluated assignment will strengthen students' academic performance and help them sharpen their writing skills more effectively.

Formative vs. Summative Assessments

When students complete a written assignment to earn a grade, they are completing a summative assessment. Another useful assessment for the purpose of measuring students' overall progress is a non-graded formative assessment. A formative assessment allows an instructor to assess a specific learning outcome, which in turn allows instructors to adapt teaching methods as needed.

Classroom Assessment Techniques: A Handbook for College Teachers (Angelo and Cross) provides an extensive collection of formative assessments. One example is the One Minute Paper. This assignment asks students to summarize their knowledge of a topic at a particular point in the class. Another non-graded formative assessment is the Muddiest Point. This asks students to identify any aspects of the class or course topics which remain unclear to them. Muddiest Points papers can also provide the basis for meaningful classroom discussions. When you include non-graded formative writing assessments, you're teaching students how to assess their own progress. This improves their critical thinking skills and also promotes cognitive development.

"Student Writing: Old Habits Die Hard, and Other Clichés"

by Kat Keifer-Newman, AdjunctNation. com, originally published April 2, 2010

Helpful Tips

Critical thinking is important, but if students can't figure out how to put their ideas down on the page in a readable way, then no one will care if they thought critically. Even if I explain all of this to the students and they agree that learning methods is what they most desire, when we get into the actual methods work they balk. No one likes to be criticized. Worse, students don't even realize they have bad habits. They believe they produce good writing.

I had a young man approach me just a few weeks ago. He shook his head, clucked his tongue, and told me that I just didn't like him and that's why I was so hard on his fantastic work. His writing was a series of long-winded sentences that offered no subject, only layers and layers of modifying adverbs and adjectives. When I asked him to find me the subject of the sentences he couldn't, of course. He was undaunted.

Denial is not new to me in these classes.

Some might think that these types of incidents are proof that students are rude and ungrateful. But I think it has more to do with how hard it is to let go of what we know, what we are comfortable with, even if that "what" doesn't gain us positive results. Change really is hard, just as the cliché goes.

Over time I've come to see that students long for their mixed metaphors, their clichés and their idiomatic phrasings. They tell me they miss randomly and unconsciously injected figures of speech. They miss their colorful phrases that they believe liven up their sentences. I patiently explain that you can't dress up bad, no matter how hard you try.

There is much hand-holding that goes on with writing assignments. Being told that one has a weak thesis, superfluous wording, poor grammar or troubled syntax can be tough. Another group will find out this week that their brilliant and clever creations are only a C- grade, at best. I regret their lost innocence, but only a little.

Getting Down To Business

Grading Written Assignments

Adult students understand they will be expected to earn a grade. A written assignment assesses their progress and their understanding of the course materials. Instructors must provide explanatory and detailed feedback to written assignments. A thorough response influences student engagement, motivation and performance.

The basis for evaluating a student's writing skills should not be focused solely on compliance, such as meeting due dates and word counts. Remember: you're concerned with addressing the students' developmental needs. Feedback that is focused only on negative aspects will discourage students.

 Start feedback on a positive note. Agood instructor always find ways to encourage students.

Here are some things to keep in mind when developing a rubric to be used for grading written assignments:

1. Start with the purpose of your class assignments. What should students accomplish through their performance or work product?

2. Consider individual strengths and areas of development.

3. Take time to explain what resources are available to meet your students' developmental needs.

4. Consider the depth of feedback provided and avoid generalizations, brief comments or canned statements.

5. Encourage students to improve their performance and offer support, guidance and responsiveness.

Students care about feedback which addresses their needs and offers suggestions for improvement. A focused approach to evaluating students' performance encourages their development, enhances their motivation and engagement in the class.

Feedback For The Exceptional Written Assignment

If you have students who have done exceptionally well on a writing assignment, how do you reward their performance? What can you offer students who demonstrate initiative and excel in their work if you have a fixed point system and extra credit is not an option? It's important to consider these questions.

When students demonstrate advanced academic skills, they can be rewarded through extended communication with the instructor. For instance, instead of corrections on a written assignment, the comments take the form of reflective questions, a dialogue between the instructor and the student. It could be accompanied by an invitation to the student to visit during office hours to continue the reflective discussion.

Another strategy that can be used to give feedback to exceptional students is peer recognition. Make certain to get the permission of the student to share portions of her/his work, and to further protect the student's privacy, remove all identifying information from the materials shared with the class or other students. This will give exceptional students an opportunity to shine (albeit privately) and the rest of the students an opportunity to elevate their own future assignments.

Regardless of the form of recognition offered for a student who has excelled, the most powerful form of acknowledgment an instructor can offer is meaningful, thoughtful feedback. Academic excellence, after all, encourages scholarly thinking.

Make Sure It's Meaningful Feedback

As an adjunct business instructor you will spend a significant amount of time providing feedback to your students, especially when it comes to written assignments. The developmental progress of your students is strengthened when you provide meaningful feedback and they respond to it. However, what do you do when students don't respond to your feedback? What if they continue to make the same mistakes and their writing does not improve? If this happens, you need to reflect on the feedback.

Getting Down To Business

First, review the comments, corrections and suggestions provided to your students. Consider your feedback is interpreted. For
example, are detailed comments more effective than one word
responses or brief comments? Are you talking at students or are
you attempting to work with them?

 Good instructors always provide supportive
comments and constructive criticism. An instructor's approach to giving feedback, along
with his or her attitude about students and their
potential, influences how students hear and
interpret feedback.

CHAPTER 10
TESTS, TESTING & ASSIGNING GRADES

Tests and Testing

There are multiple reasons for testing students. Testing communicates to the instructor whether the course objectives are being met and to what degree. Of equal importance, tests are used as an instructional tool and a learning device for students.

Test/Question Types

The major types of tests used in college classes are: essay, multiple choice and recall. In special circumstances, performance, oral and short answer tests may also be utilized.

Essay Tests/Questions

Essay tests are still one of the most popular of colleges tests, and are effective at any level of the learning hierarchy. Although essay tests require considerable time for students to respond, they provide an in-depth gauge of overall student ability. There are several factors to remember when writing test questions that require essay answers. First, essay questions should be related to the written course objectives. In addition, be certain that in terms of vocabulary, content and subject covered, the student has sufficient background to respond adequately to the question, and that the question is not ambiguous or deceptive.

Grading essay questions presents a challenge. Keep in mind essay questions ask students to be objective and justify their answers. Grade student essay question responses by listing important items expected in the response, prioritize the items, then assign more points to the highest priority items. Assigning points to the prioritized criteria will lead to more objective grades.

Getting Down To Business

Make sure essay questions do not ask for student opinions. It's extremely difficult to grade opinions rather than the student's grasp of the subject matter.

Multiple Choice Questions

With the advent of computerized scoring and large classes, multiple choice tests probably are the most used tests in college classrooms today. They are efficient in terms of time consumed, and with the use of item analysis, can determine question validity.

The development of multiple choice questions is not a simple matter. Below, you will find general guidelines for constructing multiple choice tests:

- Do not include answers that are obviously correct or incorrect or impossible responses,
- Be sure the correct answers are scattered throughout the response mechanism,
- Provide four possible responses to minimize the guess factor,
- Do not use "all of the above" or "none of the above,"
- Do not use the terms never, always, likely or similar adjectives that may divert the meaning for the student,
- Be consistent with the format so that students are not confused with wording or punctuation changes, and
- Keep choices approximately the same length since incorrect answers are frequently shorter than correct ones.

Multiple choice tests often test only the knowledge level rather than analysis and synthesis; they provide opportunity for guessing; and they depend primarily on recall and memory.

Recall and Completion Tests/Questions

Recall items may be posed as simple questions, completion or brief response. Used too often, these tests tend to encourage students to memorize rather than understand. There are, however, advantages to recall tests. They are relatively simple to grade and construct; they can address a broad field of content; and they require specific recall rather than guessing or rationalization.

Some suggestions for developing recall questions follow:

- Give information concerning the answer prior to the answer blank,
- Qualify information so students are clear about the response,
- Include responses at the analysis and synthesis level,
- Pose questions so that only one correct response is usable,
- Allow sufficient and equal space for the response,
- Avoid patterns of responses,
- Avoid direct quotes
- Avoid specific descriptors or adjectives

 True/false questions are not commonly used at the college level. Although they may have their place in a sampling of student responses or learning activity, they generally are not accepted as being objective or valid.

What Do Grades Really Measure?

What should grades really measure? This question can be answered by considering the relationship of grades to students' successful involvement and participation in the process of learning.

Getting Down To Business

As an instructor, you know that grades are the end result or final outcome for students. Perceptions about grades are often related to intended outcomes, including institutional expectations, student expectations, learning and teaching effectiveness. Instructors should use grades to measure learning, knowledge acquisition, skill set development or overall developmental growth. Grades may also reflect students' sustained efforts, their ability to read and comprehend information, and their ability to follow directions.

 Consider grades to be a cumulative measure of students progress and developmental efforts. Learning is an ongoing process measured through objectives and outcomes.

Instructors can redirect students' focus on grades by providing objective feedback addressing assignment criteria, developmental needs and the learning objectives. When detailed feedback is provided from an objective point of view, it addresses such factors as the content and mechanics of the assignment submitted. This places an emphasis on how the grade was earned. Instructors can have more impact on student outcomes by emphasizing the need to build on students' strengths and finding resources to address areas of needed development. By helping students focus on how the grade was earned and what they need to maintain or improve the resulting outcome, students learn that they have control over their grades.

For many instructors grades are a source of anxiety. Instructors should emphasize their students' learning capacity rather than the resulting grades. This perceptual shift helps the instructor view students from the perspective of what they are capable of doing. With this focus, grades are viewed as a snapshot in time when instructors are able to learn if their students are making satisfactory progress. The process of learning, knowledge creation and skill set development is ongoing and evolutionary. All students have a capacity to learn and for some students their potential to earn improved results may depend upon learning how to build on their strengths and find resources which support their progress. Learning objectives provide guidance by establishing expectations. Assessments measure students' progress towards meeting these goals.

If an instructor decides to emphasize the process of learning throughout the class, rather than focus on grades, will good grades follow? If students focus on developing their skills and improving their performance, will their resulting outcomes improve? An emphasis on getting "good grades" does not teach students to take responsibility for their own learning. It can detract from their involvement in the learning process. Instructors who encourage students to expand their capacity for learning are likely to create a supportive classroom environment which results in improved performance and participation.

As students understand what it means to do their best they are likely to receive "good grades" and more importantly, they will understand the ongoing nature of learning and the purpose of assessments. Instructors who encourage students to believe in their capabilities, while acknowledging their contributions and developmental efforts, are likely to find that they become more concerned about learning and less focused on the resulting grade received at the end of class. Grades should measure developmental progress rather than be an absolute indicator of student success. Teach students to believe in their capabilities, acknowledge their contributions and developmental efforts. They will be more concerned about what they have learned and less focused on the grade they should have or could have received by the end class.

Grading: The Basics

Grading students is probably the most difficult task for faculty. All of the elements of teaching (preparation, presentation and student activity) are reflected in the grading process. In addition, in an era of accountability, teachers are sometimes called upon to justify grades with documentation. Thus the establishment of firm criteria for grading is necessary. There are some general rules that are helpful in establishing the grading process. They are as follows:

- Communicate criteria clearly to the students.
- Include criteria other than test scores.
- Avoid irrelevant factors such as attendance and tardiness in the grading criteria.
- Place grading criteria carefully throughout the course.
- Weigh grading criteria carefully and always have a plan.
- Grade students on their achievement.

Teachers once used the technique of "grading on the curve." This placed students in competition with each other rather than cooperating in the learning experience. In the collaborative, student-centered classroom, the practice of grading on a curve is outdated.

Evaluation Plan

In order to delineate criteria for assignment of grades, develop an evaluation plan. It is a simple short worksheet form which quantifies all of the factors that apply to the evaluation.

A sample plan is shown below. Note that this type of plan allows you the freedom to assign any number of points to any criteria or activity because the final percentage will always come out to 100 percent.

Figure 10.1—Evaluation Plan

Grade Factors	Percentage of Final Grade	Possible Points	Points Received
Tests	60%	90	
Paper	20%	30	
Project	10%	15	
Class Participation	10%	15	
TOTALS	100%	150	

CHAPTER 11
TEACHING WITH TECHNOLOGY

Learning to Embrace Technological Tools

Over the past decade, there has been an evolution in class-room technology. The overhead projector, film projector and slide projector have evolved to include a Smartboard, computer, PowerPoint presentation, CD/DVD player and other multime-dia equipment. Instead of being used as props or additions to classroom teaching, technological tools are now being utilized to enhance the instructor's message and address the needs of students with a variety of learning styles. Students and many instructors rely on IT enhancements to keep everyone interested and engaged in the class.

A challenge for effective use of these tools is the time re-quired to learn and then integrate them into the classroom. It is not unusual to feel apprehension about new forms of technology. Instead of allowing yourself to feel overwhelmed, seek out train-ing classes when they are offered by your institution, either in person or online. Many companies offer online training classes or sessions in support of their products, and they often offer prod-uct manuals online. As you become comfortable with the use of new technology you are likely to try other new equipment and applications as they become available.

Since many of these tools were utilized first within organiza-tional environments and training classrooms, business instructors are likely to have an advantage and a shorter learning curve for using them in an academic environment.

Another important development for the classroom is the online learning environment. Most traditional universities offer online classes or a hybrid version that mixes on-ground and online sessions. Many bricks and mortar instructors who teach traditional classes have access to an online classroom shell to use as a means of supplementing the course with additional materials and discussion threads. Even the online classroom, utilizing a course management system, is similar in design and use to learning management systems that are developed and used in organizations. Many adjunct business instructors have a familiarity with this type of learning platform.

Technology Enhances Learning

The process of learning requires an adaptive approach by instructors and students. For instructors teaching classes on campus, the increased availability of technological tools and equipment provides an opportunity to connect in different ways with students.

The purpose of adding interactive, supplemental resources and activities and modifying teaching and instructional techniques is to make the process of learning more accessible to students of all learning styles and abilities. By offering these options, an instructor can stimulate students' interests and increase their cognitive abilities, while leading to their overall intellectual development.

Visual learners find learning is enhanced with illustrations, videos and presentations. Tactile learners connect better with interactive tools that provide a hands-on form of learning. For auditory learners, instructors should add videos or audio clips to help these students connect to the course materials.

Getting Down To Business

The online classroom does not change the principles of adult learning. Rather the format of adult learning has changed through the use of technology. The process of adult learning in any classroom environment involves the acquisition of information, interaction with that information through learning activities and the creation of new knowledge. Online students' engagement in the class is encouraged through the use of discussion boards and asynchronous interactions with their instructor.

Classroom Presentation Software

When designing multimedia instruction, the first step is the creeating learning objectives for the presentation. The final steps of the plan involves students performing tasks which integrates the information presented. The presentation software must be able to accommodate multiple forms of media, i.e., text, audio, video, graphics. Most of these forms of media are commonly used in both business and educational settings.

Presentation software affords instructors many options for demonstrating class materials and for classroom instructional options. Instructors can use presentation software, such as Microsoft PowerPoint, as a didactic aid during lectures. They also can incorporate presentation projects by students, as individuals or teams, to encourage active learning. The power of presentation software lies in its ability to incorporate a wide variety of media: text, audio, video, charts, links to websites and database files. A further element provided by presentation software is timing; all of the items presented, each "page" is referred to as a "slide," may be given a specific time signature and automated or made dependent on some action, such as a mouse click, by the presenter.

Software Applications That Enhance Learning

Many software applications can enhance on-ground lectures and the online classroom. For example, instructors may find useful games and simulations which bring the course topics and materials to life. The following is a list of additional software which can enhance the process of learning:

- Web Conferencing: This is used as a means of connecting students for a live class session online. Example: http://www.adobe.com/products/adobeconnect.html

- Wikis: This provides a means for virtual collaboration between students and/or the instructor. Example: http://www.wikispaces.com

- Jing: This software is available at no cost and allows the user to create short videos of on-screen images while narrating what is being recorded. The file is stored on the company website and a link is provided that instructors can post in the online classroom or share with their on-ground class. (http://www.techsmith.com/jing)

Integrating Social Networking into Classroom Facilitation

The use of social networking for educators has become a topic of concern because it is possible that inappropriate relationships may develop, or inappropriate postings may be viewed by students or other instructors. This does not mean that social networking should be avoided by instructors, rather the reason for its use should be first established and then all available options explored and evaluated keeping in mind an instructor's ethical obligations.

Instructors can use social networking to connect to peers, as well as to develop a community of scholars. Online instructors should explore professional networking web sites.

 Instructors should avoid integrating social networking into the classroom when a social networking site requires personal information to be shared, posted or revealed.

"Don't Poke Me: Professors' Privacy In The Age Of Facebook"

by Rich Russell, AdjunctNation.com, originally published October 22, 2010

I thought I would offer my brief note on the matter of whether to "friend" or not to "friend" one's students on Facebook. I do not—not current students anyway.

If a student requests to be my "friend" after grades have been entered for the semester (the word friend itself seems odd: are we friends? As Henry James would offer, "We are not enemies"), then I might accept, because my own page is rather tame/boring; mostly I post nothing more than links to articles (often about Facebook; how meta of me). And it is natural to feel responsible for one's students long after the term expires. It seems a good way to continue that advisory role we must undertake as educators. But while the students are still in my class or have registered for one of my classes again — why Facebook (verb) them?

Inevitably when we discuss social networking in my classes, students will ask, "Are you on Facebook, Professor Russell?" I answer, "Yes, but — do you really want me knowing what you're doing on the weekends when you should be writing papers for my class?" (Most agree not.) And while it has become selfish to want a life of one's own these days, I still do want one; does that make me a bad person, a bad professor?

I remember reading D.H. Lawrence's The Rainbow as a graduate student; I felt a great swell of empathy for the character Ursula, the schoolteacher. Ursula becomes covetous of her weekend mornings when she sits cross-stitching at home. She cannot go into town, because the students heckle her and throw stones at her on her way home. Is it so much for me to imagine the stones cast against Ursula becoming incessant pokes on Facebook?

A New Yorker article cites Facebook founder Mark Zuckerberg's affection for The Aeneid; he even quotes in the English the part about Aeneas building an empire without boundaries. But I choose to also remember Robert Frost: "who doesn't love a wall?" Is it ironic that, in maintaining my mending wall (good fences make good students), I deny current students access to my Facebook wall? But this is what I feel is appropriate; this is what I can handle right now. I leave it to others to negotiate their own privacy settings.

CHAPTER 12
TEACHING ONLINE

Getting Started

So, your teaching schedule calls for you to teach a business education course online. It doesn't matter if this is your first such venture, or you have taught at a distance before, approach the opportunity as if it were your first ever. Recall that when you decided to enter the teaching profession, you looked to the human interaction with students as a major factor in your decision. You were to be the conductor, and every class a symphony with lots of direction and emotion involved in the production (class). Now you are about to enter a new arena. As such, you must view yourself as an engineer on a train. The train has many car, each is loaded with different course delivery technologies which you will need to call upon to reach your destination (objectives). The goods you must deliver, the students, are in the last car. Sometimes, you can't even see them.

Adults interested in pursuing an advanced education are discovering that there are many more options available because of the increase in the number of online courses being offered by traditional institutions and online colleges and universities. A 2014 report published by National Center for Education Statistics revealed that as of 2012 2.6 million students were enrolled exclusively in distance education courses courses. Traditional institutions are also offering hybrid courses, which consist of a combination of physical classroom meetings and online interactions. Many for profit universities have developed online degree programs specifically to meet the needs of working adults. Businesses deliver training classes and workshops using virtual-based platforms.

Even as the number of students enrolled in online classes continues to increase, there are still questions for some educators about the ability of this environment to promote effective learning. Keep in mind that the online classroom does not change the basic principles of adult learning. An essential element of the online classroom, one that influences student motivation, engagement and performance, is the preparation and performance of the instructor. Instructors must engage students through teaching strategies and methods that are student-centered.

This chapter will provide you the skills necessary to begin your journey in the online teaching environment through the use of technology. However, as with teaching face-to-face, preparation is necessary. In fact, perhaps it's even slightly more important. In a classroom, it is easy to recover from a mishap or an error; in a distance learning situation, it is much more difficult. There are two major factors that you must keep in mind while preparing for your distance education courses: you must have complete command of the technology, and you must not lose sight of the fact that the human touch alluded to earlier is not de-emphasized, but is, in fact, emphasized as much as possible.

Master the technology, but do not get so wrapped up in it that individual students are neglected! The same basic premises apply to a distance education course; keep the lines of communication open and always be well prepared.

Online Lingo 101

Is your ISP up and your URL down? Not sure if you need to know the difference between HTTP and HTML?

On page 166 there is a glossary of the most common technical terms associated with distance education and the Internet. As a part-time faculty member assigned to teach in an online program, do you need to know all of the terms before you begin your classes? No. You will, however, come across many of these terms while teaching courses online.

Your Assignment: Skim the glossary. Stop and read the definitions of a few of the terms with which you may be familiar. Read a few of the terms you've never heard before.

Extra Credit: Incorporate the necessary terms, where appropriate, into your course description and syllabus. Make sure your students understand and use them correctly.

Traditional vs. Non-Traditional Business Students Online

The growth of online or distance learning courses and degree programs has contributed to the changing definition of "college student." "Non-traditional students" often choose online degree programs. What is the difference between a traditional and a non-traditional student? A traditional student attends college after completing high school and takes classes to prepare them for a career. Non-traditional students are adults of all ages who already have an established job or career. They seek out non-traditional forms of education, including online classes. Non-traditional students are generally working adults who are seeking professional development, skills and knowledge.

According to the National Center for Education Statistics, about half of today's students are financially independent; 49 percent are enrolled part-time; 38 percent work full-time; 27 percent have dependents of their own. Almost half, 12 million, attend two-year community colleges rather than four-year schools. Only 56 percent of students at four-year colleges complete a degree within six years, and just 20 percent of first-time students at public community colleges get a degree or certificate within three years.

 Your online classroom will consist of both traditional and non-traditional business students. Include an introductory activity at the beginning of the class to better understand your students' backgrounds and needs.

Getting Down To Business

There are many benefits to working with non-traditional students. Their experiences and perspectives help to bring business theory to life during class discussions. These students have well-defined needs, often career related, and are motivated when those needs are being met. They are also likely to be engaged in the class when they collaborate with other students. The non-traditional student is seeking meaning in the process of learning and wants to take what has been learned and apply it to career or professional goals.

When working with non-traditional students, instructors may find it necessary to reassess their facilitation methods. Students will benefit from an instructional approach that offers more than a theory-driven focus. Instructors can enhance their current teaching methods by drawing on the background that these students offer, while encouraging them to share their experiences and perspectives. Activities and assignments should encourage students to develop new insight, knowledge and real-world solutions. Online instructors can learn more about their students by requiring them to share an introduction at the start of class. By drawing upon their backgrounds and addressing their needs, an instructor can encourage development of knowledge that is relevant, meaningful and immediately applicable to their professional needs and educational goals.

Technological Preparation

When it comes to computers, count on Murphy's Law: if something can go wrong, it will. So to avoid crises ranging from delayed access to destroyed data, plan ahead. Having confidence in your tools will increase your own confidence in teaching. Here are a few tips. Share them with your students, as well:

Virus/malware protection: Virus/malware protection software is a necessity, especially if you plan to download any attachments from students onto your home computer. The two leading providers are AVG Anti-Virus (for PC) (http://free.avg.com/ww-en/free-antivirus-download) and Intego Virus Barrier (for Macintosh)

Surge protection: Be sure you have a good surge suppressor that will protect your computer during power surges and lightning strikes. For adequate protection, choose a surge suppressor with a "UL 1449" rating of at least 330V and a joule rating of at least 800V.

Computer back-ups: Be sure to back up all critical information. If you don't have a second computer, scout out computers you can use if yours fails: at your workplace, at a friend's or relative's house, at the local college or public library, or at a local internet cafe.

ISP back-ups: You also need to be prepared for your internet service to fail. It's good to have a second ISP in place for that eventuality. This webpage offers an extensive database of free ISPs by country: http://www.free-internet.name/country/United-States/ . There are also numerous libraries, cafes and restaurants that offer free Wi-Fi.

Design and Content Preparation

Inexperienced online teachers are surprised by the amount of time involved not only in creating a course, but also in facilitating it. In their 2007 research paper "What Do Online MBA Professors Have to Say About Online Teaching" authors Shijuan Liu, Kyong-Jee Kim, Curtis J. Bonk and Richard Magjuka write: "There is a general impression that online teaching and learning takes more time than traditional instruction....Not surprisingly, a number of the participants in this study mentioned the time barrier as an issue for them. A couple of faculty members, in fact, frankly stated that, 'it's just a lot of work' and 'it takes more time to teach an online course.' Additionally, one faculty member showed a specific concern about striking a balance between teaching quality and time spent on one's online classes. According to him, 'the big challenge is how I can find a way to keep the quality up and so it works for more students and it does not kill me.'"

Getting Down To Business

A 1999-2000 study conducted by Belinda Davis Lazarus, a faculty member in education at the University of Michigan-Dearborn, gives some insight into the time commitment required. Lazarus's longitudinal case study found that an experienced instructor of three online education courses spent 3.5 to 7.0 hours per week on each course. The time was spent responding to student e-mails, participating in discussions and grading.

 A significant difference in teaching a business course online is that there is much more advanced preparation necessary.

Instructors accustomed to deciding what to do in each class the night before will find the transition particularly overwhelming, for an effective and well-organized online classroom is one where all material is posted from the start. Here are some tips to help ease the transition to the online classroom:

Visit sample online classrooms to get a sense of what works and what doesn't, and to better recognize your own online teaching style. Many colleges offer sample course sites for prospective students to explore, but they're also great resources for the adjunct new to online learning. Here are a few:

- The Connecticut Distance Learning Consortium sample courses using three course management systems (WebCT, Blackboard, and WebMentor): http://www.ctdlc.org/Sample/guest.html

- University of Wisconsin: http://learn.wisconsin.edu/course.asp

- University of Wisconsin Stevens Point: http://www.uwsp.edu/natres/nres600/main.htm

- Weber State University: http://departments.weber.edu/ce/distancelearning/demo.aspx

Start simply. You don't have to incorporate all the technological bells and whistles as you begin; trying to do so will only overwhelm you. For example, if you want to incorporate live chat, but aren't sure about how it will work, you can make such interaction an option in your first course rather than a requirement.

Once you understand the technology, you'll feel better able to construct a more intricate system of group activities and discussions. "A maturity model: Does it provide a path for online course design?" (Neuhauser, 2004) identifies five levels of sophistication and qualityin online courses across five areas:

1. components and appearance

2. individualized and personal approach

3. use of technology

4. socialization and interactivity

5. assessment.

The levels of assessment, for example, would progress from no online assignments, to assignments received through e-mail, to test pools, to peer reviews, to more multi-faceted assignments.

Set tight and frequent deadlines. Consider segmenting each assignment so that one part of it is due each day. This helps prevent students from procrastinating. Make deadlines absolute, but build in crisis cushions; for example, you might allow one assignment to be turned in two days late with no penalty, but then penalize students five points for each day other assignments are late no matter what the reason.

Preparing for the start of a class should also include reviewing the assigned course materials and readings. It may be helpful to highlight key information you want to emphasize during class discussions. After reviewing the course materials you will also know if supplemental materials should be included to help students better understand the course concepts. Create a weekly preview to help students prepare for the upcoming class week.

Getting Down To Business

Consider how students will interface with the online classroom. Every course has assigned learning objectives. It is necessary to determine how students will meet those expectations and what they should demonstrate through their performance in class discussions and written assignments. By understanding how these learning goals are met, you'll be better able to assist students.

Tips For Working Efficiently

To save time, set limits on the time spent on the computer; encourage more student-to-student interaction, and make better use of time-saving technology. Here are some specific suggestions: Block out times during which you will be available to students.

- Don't respond to every student on the discussion board. Allow students to moderate discussions; they can answer each other's publicly posted questions so that the instructor isn't always expected to do so. In fact, if you respond too quickly, you can inhibit student responses.

- Have students collaborate on group projects. This results in interactions that don't involve the instructor and in fewer papers to grade.

- Save and reuse your discussion board postings from one semester to the next.

- Create a FAQ (Frequently Asked Questions) page so that you're not constantly answering the same questions.

- Use computer-graded quizzes.

- Assemble a body of internet links related to your course, and build on it each semester through your own searches, as well as by assigning students to compile and annotate a list of course-related websites.

- Have assignments due at mid-week rather than at the end of the week, especially if you want to stay away from the computer during the weekend.

- Make sure students have passed an orientation quiz or

completed an online scavenger hunt at the start of the semester so that they know how to navigate the course; this will reduce the number of questions later.

• Require that students send work as .txt (text) files if formatting is not an issue, and as .rtf (rich text format) files when formatting is important. This will minimize your download time, and problems related to software conflicts.

• Bookmark the course website, and write down the password information and tech help phone number; keep both near your computer and in your wallet for when you're working remotely.

Accessibility

Since 1998, when Congress amended the Rehabilitation Act, federal agencies have been required under Section 508 of the law to make electronic and information technology accessible to those with disabilities. Coupled with the older and more inclusive Americans with Disabilities Act, there is a greater emphasis on creating online courses that can be used by everyone.

One of the first things the part-time faculty member can do to make her/his course more accessible is to post in different formats. For example, an assignment may be posted as a Web page and also in PDF format. A lecture may be posted in text and in PowerPoint outline form, but once you've been teaching online for awhile, you'll probably want to go further. For instance, you might create HTML tags for illustrations to help the blind or avoid certain colors for those with color blindness. Look at your entire site and its ease of use for those with various disabilities. Here are some free tools that can help:

• A list of the requirements for Section 508: http://www. access-board.gov/sec508/guide/1194.22.htm

• Web Accessibility Initiative, a good overview: http://www.w3.org/WAI/Resources/

- Advice on how to design more usable Web sites: http://trace.wisc.edu/world/web/

- CynthiaSays! is a Web content accessibility validation solution, designed to identify errors in design related to Section 508 standards and the Web Content Accessibility Guidelines. This service is a free accessibility validation tester: http://www.cynthiasays.com/

- Accessibility checklist from Penn State University offers guidelines for designing or modifying Web pages for accessibility: http://accessibility.psu.edu/accessibility

- Adobe offers information and tools to make PDF files accessible: http://www.adobe.com/accessibility/tutorials.html

- Microsoft offers tutorials for using accessibility features in Windows, Word, Outlook, and Internet Explorer: http://www.microsoft.com/enable/training/default.aspx

- Vischeck allows you to see what Web sites look like for those who are color blind: http://www.vischeck.com/vischeck/

Community Building

In teaching a distance education course you are, in a sense, building your own little community. You are not just the facilitator; you are the mayor. Your #1 goal is to keep the citizens from moving out (student retention).

Attrition rates for most distance education programs,have been higher than for traditional college courses. Dropout rates are as high as 80 percent at some colleges, though this trend is changing as programs mature. Many of the reasons, such as students' inexperience with technology, or insufficient student support services, are beyond a part-timer's control. However, you can have a tremendous impact on student retention simply by the way you communicate. The form, frequency, promptness and tone of written and oral interaction with students are very important.

The trick is to create a sense of classroom community. If students feel connected, if they believe that you have a personal interest in them, they will be less likely to drop out. Research by Angie Parker, who teaches at Yavapai College, shows that those students with a higher "internal locus of control," or level of self-motivation, were more likely to complete a course. Self-motivation is a learned trait, but it develops more readily through positive reinforcement. If students in online classes feel that they are alone as they struggle with the technology and course material, they are in greater danger of dropping out. In distance education, Parker concludes, "Instructional intervention can be a powerful tool for accelerating motivational change."

The dramatic increase in the number of online courses at colleges and universities, and the problem of retaining students unprepared for this new way of learning, are leading to some research efforts aimed at systematically examining both issues. "Quality on the Line: Benchmarks for Success in Internet-Based Distance Education" (2004), a study by the Institute for Higher Education Policy, recommends that contact between faculty and students be "facilitated through a variety of ways, including voice-mail and/or email" and that "Feedback to student assignments and questions is constructive and provided in a timely manner." Communication, the study concludes, is key. In discussing community online, Gary Wheeler (Wheeler, 2002) quotes a study by Palloff and Pratt that defines the basic steps for establishing a virtual community. The steps are:

- Clearly define the purpose of the group

- Create a distinctive gathering place for the group

- Promote effective leadership within the group

- Define norms and a clear code of conduct

- Allow for a range of member roles

- Allow for and facilitate subgroups

- Allow members to resolve their own disputes.

Allowing students to resolve their own conflicts results in improved communication within the group. Since face-to-face interchange is not possible, online discussions in which students present conflicting viewpoints seem to introduce a degree of emotion into the learning process. However, you must be careful to monitor the conflict so that it does not deteriorate into personal issues and discourage dialogue.

One way to do this to set a positive tone from the start. Instructors can do this by being personal, polite, open and responsive in communications you have with individual students, and with the class as a whole. When responding to students' questions and comments on the discussion board and in email, always use their names, and consider signing messages with your first name, which seems friendlier. Make frequent use of terms like "please" and "thanks." All of this takes extra time, but it is worth it.

While it is a good idea to keep most communication on the discussion board so that you do not end up repeatedly answering the same question, e-mail can be a great tool for personal encouragement and for friendly reminders about assignments that are upcoming or overdue. To keep students on task, send weekly e-mails to those who did not post on the discussion board to let them know their contributions were missed. Another way to encourage communication is to make yourself available at times and in a manner that is most helpful for students. This doesn't mean that, as an adjunct, you need to chain yourself to your computer 24/7, but it might mean that you hold an online office hour one evening a week, perhaps the night before an assignment is due. Make it easy for students to contact you instantly, either in a chat room through the courseware or via Instant Messaging.

Group Work in the Online Classroom

The basic features of most online learning environments are quickly learned and implemented. Through time, practice and the review of training materials you can also incorporate advanced features which create a highly dynamic and interactive environment for your business students.

As noted earlier, carefully facilitated, interactive discussions promote student collaboration in the traditional classroom. In the online classroom, discussion threads provide the opportunity for collaboration. Students can develop meaningful interactions and productive communication in both environments. Within a traditional classroom an instructor easily divides up students into groups and watches interactions and progress. In the online classroom, this same process of observation is possible, provided students are required to post their communication and contributions within *dedicated* threads. For effective online group work, establish specific frameworks for group assignments and closely monitor posted interactions.

Online business students are adult learners who want to be actively involved in the process, and are willing to take responsibility for their involvement. They come to the online classroom with existing knowledge and experience that can be shared during discussions. Just as in the traditional classroom, students learn from each other even though they don't work face-to-face. In the online classroom, group assignments help students sharpen team-building, negotiation, delegation, consensus-building, and communication skills.

 In an accelerated or short term business class, there maybe not be time to implement an extensive group project. Instructors who are working with a pre-programmed set of learning activities may also not have the flexibility to incorporate additional assignments.

Practical Tips for Good Communication in Online Courses:

Helpful Tips

Call students on the phone. This is a simple and overlooked "low-tech" tool that can be very effective early in the term, especially for students who haven't gotten started yet. It's a way to show you're interested and to answer questions, usually technical, that may have them stymied.

Build a learning community. Have students post written introductions (and photographs if possible) on the discussion board—and post one yourself. Encourage students to interact with discussions about course material, either through a space on your site or in temporary chat rooms. Create an area online for socializing.

Give frequent and encouraging feedback. You might adapt the practices of a biology instructor at Piedmont Technical College in Greenwood, South Carolina, who holds online office hours, responds to email within 24 hours, gives a range of dates for an exam to be completed, and responds to students individually with their grades and where they stand in the course.

Maximize the use of the discussion board to encourage group interaction. Minimize the use of e-mail for communication, and keep communication on the discussion board as much as possible.

Check in daily to answer questions and redirect discussions if they get off track. Students need to sense your presence though you don't want to intrude. Some instructors post on discussion boards a few times during the week. Others write a weekly posting which comments directly on what students have had to say during the week. Even if a problem seems to be developing, hold back, for often the group will resolve its own conflicts and be stronger for it.

But if discussions veer wildly off track, post a follow-up question to help recapture the focus.

Be encouraging, understanding and flexible. Congratulate students on a good grade. Ask what happened when a grade was low. Allow them some time flexibility in completing assignments, if possible. Share a little of yourself. Reach out to students who are struggling. A simple note to a student asking, "Is everything OK? I haven't heard from you in a while," can give a student under great pressure the reassurance that someone cares.

Make class fun. Bramucci (2001) offers many ideas for injecting an impish spirit and for giving students reasons to check into the class more often. For example, he suggests a weekly "Guess who?" feature based on unusual facts gathered by the teacher about each student. "Hide" actual test questions on the site in a sort of "Where's Waldo?" activity. Post teasers about interesting information to be covered in an upcoming lesson. Post holiday greetings. Invite students to submit nominations for a joke of the week.

Use an Icebreaker. Maybe more so than with a class taught face-to-face, an icebreaker can be an asset for distance education classes. It commences communication immediately, gives the students a chance to participate and use the technology, and gives the instructor an opportunity to observe student writing styles.

Getting Down To Business

A Hybrid Approach to Teaching

Your institution may offer adjunct instructors online class shells to supplement traditional classrooms. The most common online course platforms include Blackboard, eCollege and Moodle. If so, consider using one of the available platforms. What are the benefits? The online class shells can increase student engagement, promote collaboration, and help to develop a sense of community.

At a very minimum create a forum in which to post course news items and updates, a thread for student questions, a forum for supplemental resources, and a forum for discussion question threads. Including these features allows students to be in contact with you and other students throughout the week, and it also provides a place for you to distribute additional handouts, website links, important updates, videos which address the course topics, and any additional materials you find helpful. If you allocate points for discussions during the traditional class sessions, you can extend that to online discussions. Some instructors make online discussions extra credit.

The addition of an online class to a traditional classroom format creates a hybrid instructional approach. Hybrid instructional methods extend an instructor's accessibility and turn weekly class sessions into week-long continuous learning events. It is not uncommon for students in a traditional classroom setting to wait to study or complete their assignments until it is close to the next class session or assignment due date. When you ask students to be involved in an online class throughout the week, you encourage them to continue working through course concepts and processing information. Offer incentives (such as extra credit) to students who are resistant to the process of online learning. However, because students are used to being involved in online social networking communities, they may not find it too difficult to utilize this environment, provided that there are meaningful learning activities and a reason for participation.

When you determine that a hybrid approach to your classroom facilitation would be beneficial, introduce students to the online class during one of your regular class meetings. If interactive presentation tools are available, demonstrate the important features and walk students through the navigational process during your class lecture to answer questions and address concerns. Explain the purpose of the online class addition (and any extra credit opportunities) as a means of encouraging student buy-in. To keep students involved and checking in on a regular basis make sure to post additional resources and frequent updates throughout the week.

By implementing a hybrid approach to classroom learning you provide another way for students to connect with the class and other students, to process information, gain new insights and perspectives. An online class module should never consist of busy work for students as they will quickly lose interest if they find there is little value in their participation with it. While there will be time involved to set it up, the end result is likely to increase interactions and engagement, which provides additional support for your students' academic development and involvement in the process of learning. Your college's Distance Learning Center will be able to provide you with ample resources for setting up a hybrid course, including tutorials in using the college's preferred online course delivery platform.

Diving Into the Wreck: Revisiting Online Classrooms After the Semester Ends

Helpful Tips

by Rich Russell, AdjunctNation.com, originally published on January 18, 2011.

It is that time, just before the new semester begins, when the online professor must again go diving into the wreck.

Well—but it was not a wreck, exactly; wreck has such a negative connotation. Something beautiful there-existed (still exists) that, after grades were entered, was allowed to drown — to quietly expire: the students denied access to the online course as the clock struck midnight at the end of the Fall term.

When a traditional class is over, it is over (done): the students hand in their final exam or final papers, exit stage-right, and that is all she wrote, so to speak. Sometimes there are frantic queries sent — desperate pleas ("oh, please, professor…!") for a clemency of additional points added. But mostly, as I admit to them on the final class when I thank them for their enthusiasm and commitment, "Some of us may never see one another again: and that is the reality of life."

Online, though, there isn't really a last class. At about this time, a week before the new semester starts, I find myself returning to those cities that were constructed over the fifteen weeks: the classrooms that have been neglected over winter break, buried in the ash. This is a return to the world of ghosts: all of those past discussions and assignments, all perfectly preserved, as if the students were still talking to one another and to me. Here one finds the truthy urn of Keats: every "LOL" and each passing disagreement frozen in a noisy yet silent form. I must admit, I find it a bit unsettling to have to revisit this place, now that the authors have all abandoned the ship, leaving me to clean up, to salvage all that worked and leave behind anything that did not.

The professor alone must return to the wreck, to turn back on the lights and have a look around before hitting the reset button.

Conclusion

I would like to thank you for reading this book. While it is meant to help both beginning and continuing faculty who teach business courses, much of the information is applicable to any college classroom. It is by no means the definitive treatise on teaching, but rather a conversation that touches on what I believe are the most important aspects necessary to teaching business and teaching business well.

Getting Down To Business

Glossary of Online Terminology

A

Adobe Acrobat Reader: A Web browser plug in program (or stand alone program) that allows you to view PDF (portable document format) files in their original format and appearance. Documents saved as .pdf files retain all their special formatting characteristics and layout properties. If you would like to provide your students with extensive printable material you may want to investigate .pdf file format. The Acrobat Reader is free and can be downloaded from Adobe.

Applet: A small Java program that can be embedded in an HTML page.

Asynchronous: Not at the same time. In an online context this term is generally used to describe various forms of communication in which participants do not have to be available at the same time (as opposed to synchronous). In online teaching, examples of common asynchronous communication includes threaded discussion (bulletin/conference) boards and email.

B

Bandwidth: Measured in Hertz (Hz). In terms of the Web it is the amount of data, usually measured in bits per second, that can be sent through a given communications channel. Bandwidth must be considered when designing Web pages as the increased requirement for bandwidth translates to increased download time for the end user. Media rich Web documents often require high bandwidth.

Bookmark: A feature of most Web browsers (called Favorites in Internet Explorer) that allows you to save frequently accessed web pages (URLs) in a special file that can be easily accessed.

Browser: A client (resides on the user's machine) software program which allow html webpages to be viewed. Common browsers are Safari, Firefox and Google Chrome. Browser software resides on the client (user's) machine.

Bulletin Board: One of the many names (others include conference board and discussion board) where asynchronous text-based online communication can occur. Many bulletin boards provide the ability for users to have threaded discussions about specific topics.

C

Cache: Browsers such as Safari, Firefox and Google Chrome hold copies of recently visited web site pages in disk memory called the cache.

Caching files in memory provides for quicker loading of files than if they are always transferred from the Web. A disadvantage of caching files is that sometimes older versions of a file loads from your computer when a newer version of the file is available on the Web. This can be particularity confusing if you are making changes to your website. Use your browser's Refresh or Reload buttons to check for more current versions of Web pages (try this before you panic).

CAI: Computer Assisted Instruction. This type of instruction uses the computer as a "teaching machine" that will present individual lessons.

Chat Room: A Chat room is a "place" where two or more individuals connected to the Internet have real-time (synchronous) conversations (usually text based) by typing messages into their computer. Groups gather to chat about various subjects. As you type, everything you type is displayed to the other members of the chat group. Some online instructors use a chat room to provide online "office hours." Students may also use a chatroom to discuss group projects or to schedule study group meetings.

Computer Conferencing: Interactive communication between networked computers in which data is shared. Data may take the form of audio, text (conference/bulletin board discussions), email, video conferencing, etc. This type of conferencing can happen in "real time," which means the messages appear as they are being typed, or they can happen asynchronously with the messages being stored for later use.

CGI: (Common Gateway Interface) A method used by WWW pages to communicate with programs run on the web server. CGI scripts are often used for interactive quizzes and data collection.

Client: A software program that is used to contact and obtain data from a Server software program on another computer. Each Client program is designed to work with one or more specific kinds of Server programs, and each Server requires a specific kind of Client. A Web Browser is a specific kind of Client software.

CMC: Computer Mediated Communication. This involves the use of computer applications that facilitate the delivery of instruction and communication such applications as email, fax, WWW.

CMI: Computer managed instruction. The computer is used to organize and track student progress as well as keep student records. CMI is often used with CAI.

D

Desktop Publishing: Preparation of printed materials such as newsletters, brochures, and business cards using the computer and specific software packages such as Adobe InDesign and Microsoft Publisher.

Distance Education: Often used interchangeably with distance learning. Typically the learners and instructors are separated by time and place. Interaction must take place through some form of media, such as print (correspondence courses) or electronic (computers). Most distance education courses use a combination of media and technologies. For example, Athabasca courses rely on a combination of print and computer.

Downloading: Transferring a file from a distant computer to a directory on your own computer.

E

Email: Electronic mail. This is a system used to send messages from one computer to another by means of a computer network. Most will allow files or documents to be "attached" for sending with the email. This is an asynchronous form of communication. It is probably the most commonly used method for distance education students to submit assignments.

Emoticon: Symbols used to convey emotions or humour, something which is difficult to do in text based communication. They are formed with specific keyboard characters. For a list go to Emoticons. Using emoticons may cause problems for people who are not aware of what the symbols mean, careful use of the written word may be a better way to communicate :-).

F

F2F (or f2f): Abbreviation for face-to-face. This describes the traditional classroom setting.

FAQ: A list of Frequently Asked Questions and their answers.

FTP: File Transfer Protocol allows computer data to be transferred between computers. FTP is a special way to login to another Internet site for the purposes of retrieving and/or sending files. There are many Internet sites that have established publicly accessible repositories of material that can be obtained using FTP, by logging in using the account name anonymous, thus these sites are called anonymous FTP servers.

G

GIF: Graphics Interchange Format. One format for image compression. Images placed on web pages are usually in GIF or JPEG format. GIFs are generally used for images with 256 or fewer colours (line drawings, for example).

H

Home page: The home page is generally the first page of a web site and often acts as the information center for the entire site. From the home page, users can navigate to other web pages within the web site. Home pages are often named "index.html" or "default.html"

HTML: HyperText Markup Language. A set of codes which must be used in documents to be accessed on the WWW. Without them the page would not be readable in the browser.

HTTP: Hypertext Transfer Protocol. This is used to indicate that an Internet site is part of the WWW. It is found in the web address. http://members.home.net/.

Hypertext: Text and/or images which a user can click on to be connected to other information within the same site and/or other sites.

I

Internet: The largest international network of interconnected computers. This is made up of numerous smaller networks linked together by TCP/IP protocols.

Internet Courses: Students use the Internet to participate in their coursework. Relevant information and assignments are posted to the Web by the instructor. Communication is usually by email, discussion boards, chat, etc.

Internet Explorer: A web browser software that was developed by Microsoft.

ISP: Internet Service Provider. This is an organization whose business is to provide access to the Internet in some form, usually with a monetary charge attached.

J

Java: Java is a network-oriented programming language invented by Sun Microsystems that is specifically designed for writing programs that can be safely downloaded to your computer through the Internet and immediately run without fear of viruses or other harm to your computer or files. Using small Java programs (called "Applets"), Web pages can include functions such as animations, calculators, and other fancy tricks.

JavaScript: JavaScript was developed by Netscape and is a scripting language that allows one the ability to embed script into Web pages. JavaScripts can be used to add some interactive features to Web pages (an example is the roll over effect you see with the navigation buttons on this web site). JavaScript and Java are two different programming languages.

JPEG: Joint Photographic Experts Group. One format for image compression. Images placed on web pages are often in GIF or JPEG format. JPEG compression is generally used for photographs or pictures/graphics that use more than 256 colours.

K

Kilo: Abbreviated "k". It means one thousand. In computer specifications it has an exact value of 1,024. It is used when talking about size of memory or hard drive storage space.

KBps: Kilobytes per second.

L

Link: An area within a website document which can be clicked on to transfer the viewer to more information within the same website or to another site.

Listserv: The most common kind of mail list.

Logging on: The process of connecting to a computer network. It usually involves the use of a password.

Lurking: A person is lurking if they read postings to bulletin boards but rarely if ever respond or post comments to the bulletin board themselves. This person would be analogous to the person who sits in a classroom and listens but rarely speaks.

M

Markup: A type of coding used in creating web documents. It is used to create the format and/or links. Common forms are HTML and SGML.

Getting Down To Business

MIME: Multipurpose Internet Mail Extensions. The email standard that allows you to send and receive (via email) non-text files as attachments to standard Internet mail messages. Non-text files include graphics, spreadsheets, formatted word-processor documents, sound files, etc.

If you are teaching online you will want both your email software and your student's email software set up to be MIME compliant.

Modem: (MOdulator, DEModulator) An electronic device that allows computers to interact by converting computer data into an audio signal which can be sent over a telephone line.

MPEG: Moving Picture Experts Group. A compression and storage standard for motion video.

N

Netiquette: The etiquette on the Internet. For some guidelines and some core rules check out this Netiquette web page. If you would like to test your own netiquette try out this Netequitte Quiz."

Network: A number of computers which are linked together allowing exchange of data and sharing of resources.

Newsgroup: A discussion forum, similar to bulletin board postings, about specific topics. Many of the newsgroups have worldwide distribution. Contributors post messages for others to read and respond to.

As an online teacher, you may want to investigate using newgroups related to your field or discipline.

O

Online: You have access, and are connected to, a computer network (usually the Internet).

P

Password: A code used to gain access to a locked system. A good password should be made up of a combination of letters and numbers and/or symbols. It should not be an easy combination or something commonly associated with the user.

Plug-in: A piece of software, usually fairly small, that adds a feature or features to a larger piece of software. It is downloaded to the computer's memory. The user can choose which plug-ins to download from a large number available. Examples of common plug-ins are RealAudio, QuickTime, and Adobe Reader.

Posting: A message put into a network communication system such as a bulletin board.

Protocol: The standard used which allows computers and networks to communicate with each other.

Q

Quicktime: A multimedia software that was developed by Apple. It delivers synchronized media such as graphics, sound, video and text.

R

Real Time: Information is received and responded to with no time delay. See Synchronous.

S

Search Engine: Allows the user to search for specific content defined by the user. It can be set up to search within a web site or the whole Internet. Common ones are Yahoo, Ask.com, Google and Bing.

Server: A networked computer or software package that allows client software running on client machines the ability to access remote (to the client) services or information. An example is a Web server and web server software which allows you to access this web site.

SGML: Standard Generalized Markup Language. HTML is a form of this international standard for electronic markup language.

Spam (or Spamming): The use of electronic communication (often email) to broadcast unsolicited messages to others.

Streaming: Video and/or sound is played in real time as it is downloaded over the Internet. It is played by a web browser plugin as it is transferred to the computer. Since it is not stored as a file on your computer, a fast Internet connection and powerful computer are necessary.

Synchronous: Opposite of asynchronous. In an online context this term is generally used to describe communication between individuals in real time but who are not in the same place. Chat lines are an example of this.

T

T-1: A high speed (1.544 Mbps (million bits/second)) carrier of digital or voice data. It has 24 voice channels.

T-3: A digital channel which is significantly faster than T-1 (45.304 Mbps).

TCP/IP: The Transmission Control Protocol (TCP) and the Internet Protocol (IP) are protocols that let different types of computers communicate with each other.

Teleconferencing: A two way communication between two or more people who are in different locations. This can be via video, audio, or computer systems.

U

URL: Uniform Resource Locator. This is basically an address for a website on the World Wide Web. An example of a URL is http://cde.athabascau.ca/ (The home page for Athabasca University's Centre for Distance Education).

V

Video Conferencing: A communication occurring between two or more remote locations that includes video and audio contact.

Getting Down To Business

W

Web page: A site which can be found on the World Wide Web (WWW) by it's URL. It will contain data which has been written into a file and stored on a server. Web pages for distance education courses may contain such items as the course syllabus, course materials and assignments and links to resources for the course.

WWW: The World Wide Web is a vast collection of information (and mis-information) which can be accessed by anyone who is "hooked up" to the Internet.

X

XML: Extensible Markup Language. An extremely simple dialect of SGML for use on the WWW.

Y

Yahoo: One of the largest hierarchical indices of the WWW. It can be used to search for sites on the WWW. (Is short for Yet Another Hierarchical Organized Oracle)

Yottabyte: 2^{80} = 1,208,925,819,614,629,174,706,176 bytes. (Just in case you wanted to know!)

Z

Zettabyte: 2^{70} = 1,180,591,620,717,411,303,424 bytes. (Just in case you wanted to know!)

References

America Association of University Professors. 2009. "Statement on Professional Ethics." Retrieved June 2, 2013 from the World Wide Web: <http://www.aaup.org/report/statement-professional-ethics>

Angelo, T.A. 1991. "Learning in the classroom (Phase I)." A report from the Lawrence Hall of Science, University of California at Berkeley, California.

Angelo T. & Cross K. 1993. *Classroom Assessment Techniques: A Handbook for College Teachers* (2nd ed.). San Francisco: Jossey-Bass.

Atkinson, M., Wilson, T., and Kidd, J. 2008. "Virtual education: teaching and learning in Second Life." *Teaching and Learning in Higher Education*, 50:1.

Bakker, C., Fennimore, T.F., Fine, C., Jones, B.F., Pierce, J., Tinzmann, M.B., 1990. *What Is the Collaborative Classroom?* Oak Brook Press.

Beck, E. 2008. *Going the Distance: A Handbook for Adjunct & Part-Time Faculty Who Teach Online, 1st Edition.* Ann Arbor: Part-Time Press.

Bianco-Mathis, V. et al. 1996. *The Adjunct Faculty Handbook.* Thousand Oaks, CA: Sage Publications, Inc.

Bligh, D.A. 1971. *What's the Use of Lectures?* Exeter, Devon: D.A., and B. Bligh.

Bligh, D. A. 2000. *What's the Use of Lectures?* San Francisco: Jossey-Bass.

Bloom, B. et. al. 1956. *Taxonomy of Educational Objectives.* New York: David McKay.

Bonk, C.J., Kim Kyong-Jee, Liu Shijuan and Magjuka, R. 2007. "What Do Online MBA Professors Have to Say About Online Teaching." Retrieved June 2, 2013 from the World Wide Web: <http://www.westga.edu/~distance/ojdla/summer102/liu102.htm>

Bramucci, R. 2001. "Ideas for distance learning." Retrieved September 11, 2004 from the World Wide Web: <http://fdc.fullerton.edu/learning/STG2001_IDEAS.htm>.

Brownstein, E., and Klein, R. 2006. "Blogs — applications in science education." *Journal of College Science Teaching*, XXXV, 6:18-22.

Burnstad, H. 2000. "Developing the environment for learning." In Greive D, (ed.). *Handbook II-Advanced Teaching Strategies for Adjunct and Part-time Faculty.* Ann Arbor, MI: Part-Time Press.

Cann, A., Badge, J., Johnson, S., and Moseley, A. 2009. "Twittering the students experience." *Association for Learning Technology Online Newsletter,* Issue 17, Monday, 19 October, 2009.

Center for Community College Student Engagement. 2007. Community College Survey of Student Engagement, <http://www.ccsse.org/> .

Collins, Dr. Michael. 2011. *Teaching in the Sciences: A Handbook for Part-Time & Adjunct Faculty.* Ann Arbor: Part-Time Press.

Cooper, J.L., and Robinson, P. 2000. "The argument for making large classes seem small." *New Directions for Teaching and Learning.* 81, 63-76.

de Fondeville, T. 2009. "Ten steps to better student engagement." Edutopia.com <http://www.edutopia.org/project-learning-teaching-strategies.>

Duncan, D. 2005. *Clickers in the Classroom: How to Enhance Science Teaching Using Classroom Response Systems.* San Francisco: Pearson Education/Addison-Wesley/Benjamin Cummings.

Eisner, S. 2004. "Teaching generation Y college students: three initiatives." *Journal of College Teaching and Learning,* 1(9) , 69-84.

ERIC Digest, 2005 "It Takes a Village: Academic Dishonesty & Educational Opportunity." <http://www.eric.ed.gov/ERICWebPortal/detail?accno=EJ720381>

Erickson, B.L., and Strommer, D.W. 1991. *Teaching College Freshmen.* San Francisco: Jossey-Bass.

Fletcher, A. 2009. "Defining student engagement: A literature review." SoundOut.org <http://www.soundout.org/student-engagement-AF.pdf.>

Garner, H. 2011. *Frames of Mind: The Theory of Multiple Intelligences.* New York, NY: Basic Books.

Greenhow, C. 2012. *Twitteracy: Tweeting as a New Literacy Practice.* The Educational Forum, 76: 463–477.

Greive, D. (Ed.). 2010. *A Handbook for Adjunct/Part-time Faculty & Teachers of Adults.* Ann Arbor, MI: Part-Time Press.

Greive, D. (Ed.). 2000. *Handbook II-Advanced Teaching Strategies for Adjunct and Part-time Faculty.* Ann Arbor, MI: Part-Time

References

Press.

Guthrie, R.W., and Carlin, A. 2004. "Waking the dead: using interactive technology to engage passive listeners in the classroom." Proceedings of the Tenth Americas Conference on Information Systems, New York.

Hartley, J., and Davies, I.K. 1978. "Note-taking: a critical review." *Programmed Learning and Educational Technology*, 15, 3, 207-224.

Heppner, F. 2007. *Teaching the Large College Class: A Guidebook for Instructors with Multitudes.* San Francisco: Jossey-Bass.

Herreid, C.F. 2006. "Clicker" cases: introducing case study teaching into large classrooms." *Journal of College Science Teaching,* XXXVI, 2,43-47.

Johnson, B. 2010, November. Blog entry: "Student engagement—why it matters, parts I, II, III." <http://www.AdjunctNation.com>

Jones, R. 2008. "Strengthening student engagement." International Center for Leadership in Education. <http://www.leadered.com/pdf/Strengthen%20Student%20Engagement%20white%20paper.pdf.>

Knowles, M. 1990. *The Adult Learner-A Neglected Species.* Houston, TX: Gulf Publishing.

Lay, Robert. 2000. "Demographic change and emerging talent pools." *Company Magazine.* 42, 53-60.

Lazarus, B. D. "Teaching courses online: How much time does it take?" *Journal of Asynchronous Learning Networks,*7(3). Retrieved November 9, 2004 from the World Wide Web: <http://www.sloan-c.org/publications/jaln/v7n3/v7n3_lazarus.asp>.

Lewis, K.G. 1994. "Teaching large classes (How to do it well and remain sane)." In Prichard, K.W., and Sawyer, R.M. (eds.). *Handbook of College Teaching: Theory and Application,* p. 319-343. London: Greenwood Press.

Lloyd, D.H. 1968. "A concept of improvement of learning response in the taught lesson." *Visual Education,* October, 23-25.

Mager, R. 1962. *Preparing Instructional Objectives.* Belmont, CA: Fearon Publishers.

McCarthy, B. 1987. *The 4-MAT System.* Barrington, IL: Excel, Inc.

McKeachie, W. et. al. 1994. *Teaching Tips, Srategies, Research and Theory for College and University Teachers.* Lexington, MA: D. C. Heath and Co.

McLeish, J. 1968. *The Lecture Method. Cambridge Monographs on Teaching Methods.* Cambridge, U.K.: Cambridge Institute of Education.

NEA, 1975. <www.new.org/aboutnea/code.html.>

Neuhauser, C. "A maturity model: Does it provide a path for online course design?" *Journal of Interactive Online Learning,* 3(1). Retrieved August 30, 2004 from the World Wide Web: <http://www.ncolr.org/jiol/issues/>.

New England Literacy Resource Center, 2009. "Drivers of persistence." <http://www.nelrc.org/persist/drivers_belonging.html>

Palloff, R. M., & Pratt, K. 2003. *The Virtual Student: A Profile and Guide to Working with Online Learners.* San Francisco: Jossey-Bass.

Palmer, C. 2009. "Building student engagement: classroom atmosphere." FacultyFocus.com <http://www.facultyfocus.com/articles/effective-classroom-management/building-student-enga.>

Parker, A. "Identifying predictors of academic persistence in distance education." *USDLA Journal,17(1).* Retrieved November 9, 2004 from the World Wide Web: <http://www.usdla.org/html/journal/JAN03_Issue/article06.html>.

Phipps, R. "Quality on the line: Benchmarks for success in Internet-based distance education." 2000. The Institute for Higher Education Policy. Retrieved August 30, 2004 from the World Wide Web: <http://www.ihep.com/Pubs/PDF/Quality.pdf>.

Ruhl, K.L., Hughes, C.A., and Schloss, P.J. 2007. "Using the Pause Procedure to enhance lecture recall." *Teacher Education and Special Education,* 10(1),14-18.

Russell, R. 2011, January. Blog entry: "Diving Into the Wreck: Revisiting Online Classrooms After the Semester Ends" <http://www.AdjunctNation.com>

Salomon, J. 1994. "The diverse classroom." In Frye, B. (ed). *Teaching in College-A Resource for College Teachers.* Elyria OH: Info-Tec.

San Francisco State University. *The Center for Teaching and Faculty*

References

Development, 2013. *<http://ctfd.sfsu.edu/>*

Sego, A. 1994. *Cooperative Learning-A Classroom Guide*. Elyria, OH: Info-Tec.

Schreyer Institute for Teaching Excellence. Teaching Large Classes, 2013. *<http://www.schreyerinstitute.psu.edu/Tools/Large/>*

Stephan, K., 2000. "The syllabus and the lesson plan." In Greive, D. (ed). *Handbook II-Advanced Teaching Strategies for Adjunct and Part-time Faculty*. Ann Arbor, MI: Part-Time Press.

Tinzmann, M.B., Jones, B.F., Fennimore, T.F., Bakker, J., Fine, C., and Pierce, J. 1990. "What Is the Collaborative Classroom?" North Central Regional Educational Laboratory (NCREL), Oak Brook.

Umbach, P.D. "The effects of part-time faculty appointments on instructional techniques and commitment to teaching." Paper Presented at the 33rd Annual Conference of the Association for the Study of Higher Education, Jacksonville, FL, November 5-8, 2008.

University of Oregon. Teaching Effectiveness Program, 2013. <http://tep.uoregon.edu/resources/faqs/issuesofrespect/positiverelate.html>

Weaver, R.L., and Cotrell, H.W. 1987. "Lecturing: essential communication strategies." In Weimer, M.G. (Ed.). *Teaching Large Classes Well. New Directions for Teaching and Learning*, no. 32, 57-69. San Francisco: Jossey-Bass.

Weimer, M. 1990. *Improving College Teaching*. San Francisco: Jossey-Bass.

Wheeler, Gary S. 2002. *Teaching and Learning in College* (4th ed.). Ann Arbor, MI: Part-Time Press.

Wulff, D. H., Nyquist, J. D., & Abbott, R. D. 1987. "Students' perceptions of large classes." In K. E. Eble (Series Ed.) & M. G. Weimer (Vol. Ed.), *New Directions for Teaching and Learning*: Vol. 32. *Teaching Large Classes Well*. San Francisco: Jossey-Bass.

Yazedjian, A., and Kolkhorst, B.B. 2007. "Implementing small-group activities in large classes." *College Teaching*, 55(4), 164-169.

Index

Symbols

4mat system 38

A

academic dishonesty 31,32 *See also* plagiarism
accessibility 31,32
accountability 13,31,32,106,139
active learning 31,32,45,87
AdjunctNation.com 11,113,131,146,164
adult leaner*See* adult students
adult students 9,13,23,26,38,40,47,51,57,68,71,94
affective domain 31,32,46,47
American Association of University Professors 30
Americans with Disabilities Act 31,32,155
amplitude 31,32
analog 31,32,166
andragogy 37,57
anecdotes 14,20,23,24,26,27,45,70,106
Angelo, T.A. 87,173
assessments 20,51,62,84,130,139
Assessment Update 57
assignments 14,15,33,36,43,48,50,62,64,66,73,87,99,102,110,111,115,116,
    121,124,125,126,127,128,132,133,150,153,154,157,158,159,161,162
asynchronous 144
Atkinson, M. 81,173
attrition 156
AVG Anti-Virus 150

B

Bakker, J. 67,177
barriers 46,66
B.F. Jones 67
Blackboard 81,152,161
Bligh, D.A. 87,90,173
blogging 78
blogs 79,81,120
Bloom, Benjamin 46
Bloom's Taxonomy of Educational Objectives 46
Bolton, Fred C. 57

Bonk, Curtis J. 151
Bramucci, R. 161,173
Brownstein, E. 173
Burnstad, Helen 19
business classes 16,75,119
business students 15,18,95,149,158
buzz groups 24

C

CAI*See* computer assisted instruction
Carlin, Anna 83
case studies 17,42,48,56
Center for Academic Integrity 32
Center for Teaching and Faculty Development 122,176
Fine, C. 67
cheating 31,32
class discussions 15,17,34,35,49,51,54,62,69,75,92,96,108,115,150,153
class expert (student type) 70
classroom behavior 28,69
clickers 82,84,120,122
Code of Ethics of the Education Profession 30
cognitive domain 46
collaborative learning 24,42,44,64,96
communication 15,16,19,21,23,24,25,26,29,34,38,39,44,63,69,71,72,74,78,
96,97,111,119,133,148,158,159,160
community building 156
community-centered learning 18
Community College Survey of Student Engagement 59
Computer Assisted Instruction *See* CAI
conflict 52,55,96,158
conflict management 158
Connecticut Distance Learning Consortium 152
content preparation 151
cooperative learning 38,65
Cooper, J.L. 115
copyright 27
Cottrell, H.W. 118
course content 45
course description 28,103,149
course goals 102
course management 143,152
course objectives 21,33,46,70,125,135
course outline 33,106
critical thinking 16,18,24,38,42,46,49,50,56,62,92,125,130

Cross, Patricia 130
Cruce, Ty M. 65

D

databases 10
Davies, I.K. 89
de Frondeville, Tistan 63
demonstration 82,83,86,87,90
descriptors 137
Desire2Learn 81
discussion board 154,158,160
distance education 13,82,148,156,157,161
diversity 45
download 43,150,155
Gardner, Howard D. 40
Duncan, D. 83

E

eCollege 161
educational mission 14
email 33,81,99,102,120,153,157,158,160
engagement 12,35,51,60,62,63
Engagement 35,59
ERIC 32
Erickson, B.L. 100
essay 103,121,135,136
ethical issues 27,29
evaluation 26,28,31,46,93,98,102,111,126,140
evaluation form 98
evaluation, in cognitive domain 46
evaluation plan 31,140,141
evaluation procedures 102
evaluation, student 31
exams 31,102,103,104,108,117,121

F

Facebook 78,81,146
facilitation 36,41,55,60,62,68,71,72,77,98,108,150
facilitator of learning 26,37,66,95
FAQ 154
feedback 16,34,36,38,44,52,55,56,64,69,73,74,75,80,83,98,103,117,120,
     125,128,132,133,134,138,160
feedback mechanism 44
Fennimore, T.F. 67

field trips 18,87
Fine, C. 67
first class 14,23,32,38,71,99,100,111,112,115
Fletcher, Adam 64
Freeway Flyers 11

G

Gardner's Multiple Intelligences 27
grading 33,98,121,132,139,140,152
grading policy 33,98
Greenhow, Christine 79
group activities 24,153
group discussions 24,90,119
group project 61,95,154,159
group strategies 46
group work 38,51,70,95,96,97,122,159
guest speaker 18
Guthrie, R.W. 83

H

handouts 22,33,86,107,117,162
Hartley, J. 89
Heppner, F. 121
Herreid, C.F. 84
homework 117,122,124,125
host 82
HTML 148,155
HTTP 148
humor 23,26
hybrid classes 161

I

icebreaker 100,161
Inductive learning 87
Institute for Higher Education Policy 157
institutional goals 106
instructional methods 86,162
instructional objectives 13
Intego Virus Barrier 150
interactivity 117,153
Internet 10,27,87,154,156,157
ISP 148,151
item analysis 136

J

Jing 145
Jones, B.F. 67
Jones, Richard D. 62
Journal of Higher Education, The 57,65
J. Pierce 67
J. Solomon 45

K

Keifer-Newman, Kat 131
Kidd, J. 82
Kinzie, Jillian 65
Klein, Ezra 79
Knowles, Malcolm 37
Kolb Learning Style Inventory 41
Kolkhorst, B.B. 117
Kuh, George D. 57,65
Kyong-Jee, Kim 151

L

large classes 82,102,114,115,118,121,122,123,136
Lazarus Davis, Belinda 152
learning college 18
learning community 160
learning management systems 143
learning objectives 10,34,35,43,48,50,62,98,109,128,138,144
learning styles 25,38
lecture 45,82,84,86,87,88,89,91,95,96,101,108,109,112,113,115,116,117,
        118,155,162
lecture 87,88
legal issues 29
lesson plan 26,45,70,93,106,107
Lewis, T. 101,115
live chat 153
Lloyd, D.H. 88

M

Magjuka, Richard 151
malware 150 *See also* virus protection
Maslow's Hierarchy of Needs 52,53
M.B. Tinzmann 67
McAfee 150
McKeachie, W. 27

McLeish, J. 88
Michigan State University 79
Miller, Melissa 113
minute paper 120,130
Moodle 161
motivation 115,157
Muddiest Point 130
multimedia 86
multiple choice 82,135
Multiple Intelligences 40
Myers Briggs Type Indicator 40
MySpace.com 81

N

National Center for Education Statistics 147,149
National Education Association 30
National Survey of Student Engagement 74
negative student (student type) 70
networks 79
Neuhauser, C. 153
New England Literacy Resource Center 63
non-electronic response systems 84
nontraditional students 149

O

office hours 29,82,99,101,160
off-the-subject student 70
online classrooms 152
open-ended questions 24
Ortiz, Jenny 11

P

Parker, Angie 157
pedagogy 37,115
peer review 153
Piedmont Technical College 160
Pierce, J. 67
plagiarism 31,32,102,110
planning for teaching 99
PowerPoint 99,116,119,142,144,155
Problem-based learning 87
problem-solving 24

projects 41,66,67,77,87,95,121,122,127,144,154
projects, student 66,67
psychomotor domain 46

Q

question-and-answer 86
questioning 70
question validity 136

R

Rehabilitation Act 155 *See also* accessibility
reinforcement 20,24,70,157
research 12,13,16,17,18,29,31,42,44,50,58,59,60,78,87,99,126
Russell, Rich 146,164
Robinson, P. 115
rubric 57,127,128,132
Ruhl, K.L. 89

S

San Francisco State University 122
Schreyer Institute for Teaching Excellence 123
search engines 27
Second Life 81
Shijuan, Liu 151
Shoup, Rick 65
Sloan Consortium 147
social networking 28,81,145,146,162
software 33,81,82,107,111,116,144,145,150,155
Solomon, J. 45
Stephan, W. 107
stereotyping 45
Strommer, D.W. 100,101
student attention 88
student-centered learning 19,41
student engagement 60,61,65
student evaluation 31
student motivation 36,52,148
student panels 24
student participation 23,31
student response systems*See* clickers
student retention 58,59,60,71,156
student success 65
styles of teaching 25
supplemental materials 43,108,109,153

syllabus 20,33,41,99,102,106,125,149

T

teacher behaviors 19,66
teaching goals 19
teaching strategies 44,70,86
teaching styles 25,26
technology 67,82,86,116,148,153,154,155,157,161
testing 83,121,135
tests 31,33,81,82,89,99,108,109,110,116,121,135,136,137
textbooks 107
Fennimore, T.F. 67
the negative student 70
the off-the-subject student 70
the quiet class 70
the talkative class 70
the unruly student 70
Three R's of Teaching 24
time management 77
time management plan 77
time-on-task 20
Tinzmann, M.B. 79
traditional students 149
transformational learning 37,50,51
Tweet 80
Twitter 78,79,80,81,120

U

Umbach, P.D. 60
Universal Design for Learning 122
University of California at Berkeley 87
University of Leicester 79
University of Michigan-Dearborn 152
University of Oregon 73
University of Wisconsin 152
University of Wisconsin Stevens Point 152
URL 148

V

VARK 40
virus protection 150
voice over internet protocol 81
VoIP 81

W

Weaver, R.L. 118
web conferencing 144
WebCT 152
Weber State University 152
WebMentor 152
What's the Use of Lectures 88
Wheeler, Gary 157
Wikis 145
Wilson, L.D. 82
Wilson, T. 81
written assignments 15,16,49,121,124,125,126,127,128,132,133

Y

Yavapai College 157
Yazedjian, A. 117
YouTube.com 81

If you found this book helpful, you'll want to check out these other titles:

Handbook II: Advanced Strategies for Adjunct and Part-time Faculty by Donald Greive

Handbook II: Advanced Teaching Strategies carries on the tradition of practical and readable instructional guides that began with *A Handbook for Adjunct & Part-time Faculty* (now in its 7th edition!)

Intended for adjuncts who have already mastered the basics and for the managers of adjunct faculty, *Handbook II: Advanced Teaching Strategies* offers in-depth coverage of some of the topics you just read about like andragogy, collaborative learning, syllabus construction, and testing. But this manual also goes beyond these topics to discuss specific teaching techniques for critical thinking, problem solving, large class instruction and distance learning assignments.

Handbook II: Advanced Teaching Strategies gives you expert and current strategies to take your teaching to the next level. Available in paperback for $20.00 each. Digital e-book: $10.

A Handbook for Adjunct/Part-Time Faculty & Teachers of Adults, Seventh Edition by Donald Greive

This is more than just a teacher's manual! This little powerhouse helps adjuncts tackle the day-to-day problems associated with teaching part-time. From course planning to teaching adult students, this book offers practical suggestions, strategies and advice. With over 250,000 copies sold, *A Handbook* provides adjuncts with the contents of a first-rate teaching workshop for a fraction of the price. Available in paperback for $20.00 each.

NOTE: *A Handbook & Handbook II* are available in a set for $35 per set. Digital e-book set: $18.

FAQ's...

How can I place an orders?

Orders may be placed **by mail** to Part-Time Press, P.O. Box 130117, Ann Arbor, MI 48113-0117, **by phone** at (734)930-6854, **by fax** at (734)665-9001, and **via the Internet** at http://www.Part-TimePress.com.

How much do I pay if I want multiple copies?

The Part-Time Press offers a generous multiple copy discount:
1-9 copies no discount   **10-49 copies** 10% discount
50-99 copies 20% discount   **100 + copies** 30% disocunt

How can I pay for orders?

Orders can be placed on **a purchase order** or can be paid by **check** or **credit card** (Visa/Mastercard, Discover or AMEX.)

How will my order be shipped?

Standard shipping to a continental U.S. street address is via **UPS-Ground Service**. Foreign shipments or U.S. post office box addresses go through the **U.S. Postal Service** and express shipments via **UPS-2nd Day**, or **UPS-Next Day**. Shipping and handling charges are based on the dollar amount of the shipment, and a fee schedule is shown on the next page.

What if I'm a reseller like a bookstore or wholesaler?

Resellers get a standard **20 percent discount** off of the single copy retail price, or may choose to receive the multiple copy discount.

Part-Time Press Books: Order Form

Qty	Title	Unit $$	Total
	Handbook for Adjunct/Part-Time Faculty, 7th ed.	$20.00	
	Handbook II: Advanced Teaching Strategies	$20.00	
	Going the Distance: A Handbook for Part-Time & Adjunct Faculty Who Teach Online, Rev. 1st ed.	$15.00	
	Teaching in the Sciences	$20.00	
	Getting Down to Business	$20.00	
	Teaching Strategies and Techniques, 5th ed.	$15.00	
	Teaching & Learning in College	$20.00	
	The Undergrad Library Collection (7 book collection)	$115.00	
		Subtotal	
		Shipping	

Shipping Schedule:

1-4 books   *$6.00*

5+ books   *8 percent of the purchase price*

Part-Time Press: P.O. Box 130117, Ann Arbor, MI 48113-0117
Ph: 734-930-6854 Fax: 734-665-9001 E-mail: orders@part-timepress.com
Order securely online: http://www.Part-TimePress.com/shop

Purchaser/Payment Information

☐ Check (payable to The Part-Time Press)

☐ Credit Card # ———————————————— Exp.————

  CVV# ————

☐ Purchase Order # ————————————————

Name ————————————————————————

Institution ——————————————————————

Address ————————————— City/ST/Zip ——————————

Ph:———————————— Email: ————————————

Getting Down To Business

Getting Down To Business